Those Immigrants!

Indians in America: A Psychological Exploration of Achievement

Published by
FiNGERPRINT!
An imprint of Prakash Books India Pvt. Ltd.

113/A, Darya Ganj, New Delhi-110 002
Tel: (011) 2324 7062 – 65, Fax: (011) 2324 6975
Email: info@prakashbooks.com/sales@prakashbooks.com

facebook www.facebook.com/fingerprintpublishing
twitter www.twitter.com/FingerprintP, www.fingerprintpublishing.com
For manuscript submissions, e-mail: fingerprintsubmissions@gmail.com

ISBN: 978 81 7599 373 0

Processed & printed in India

Those Immigrants!

Indians in America: A Psychological Exploration of Achievement

SCOTT HAAS

FiNGERPRINT!

DEDICATION

For Laura, At Last and Always,
and For Taking Me to India
in the First Place

Contents

OUR JOURNEY CONTINUES: THE PUBLIC GOOD, MORE MOVIES, THE PHILOSOPHER OF WALL STREET, A MEDIA MOGUL, AND AN ANALYTIC JOURNALIST 131

**WE CONCLUDE OUR TRIP FOR NOW WITH
EDUCATORS, THE NEXT GENERATION,
A PSYCHOLOGIST, MEDIA GENIUSES,
THE MAN FROM PHILADELPHIA,
AND A SONG FOR TOMORROW** **233**

FOREWORD

In 1958, my father boarded a plane to journey to America, leaving my mother and older brother back in India. He came to America, like generations of immigrants, looking for opportunity and the chance to create a better life and future. Soon after, my mother and brother followed, and they all settled in California. My father became an engineer, my mother a public school teacher. A second brother was born in 1961, and my story began in 1965.

The year 1965 was an important one in American history, certainly, but it was also a pivotal year in the story of the Indian American diaspora. Over the next ten years, I saw aunts and uncles, cousins and family friends arrive in America. Most were here to pursue their education, but some were also starting small businesses, from family run motels to liquor stores and gas stations to early technology and medical firms. And I'd emphasize the word *family*. Everyone chipped in where they could, putting everything back into whichever endeavour that person was engaged in. It was a group effort. And this Indian American story was not just playing out in my family, but in countless families throughout the United States.

As the first generation born in America, I was the typical American kid. Boy Scouts, little league, student council, and weekends helping out at the family motel. But underlying this were core principles that my parents instilled in my brothers and me. *Work hard. Education is the key to success. Your family will always be there for you. Give back to your community. Don't be afraid to try.* And, oh yes, *become a doctor.*

I must have listened . . . I got good grades, went to medical school and became a doctor, had a successful career in medicine—going from practice to helping run a five hospital health system to being the chief medical officer for Sacramento County and an associate dean at the University of California, Davis. And in 2013, standing on the floor of the House of Representatives I got sworn in as a Member of Congress. I remember looking up into the gallery and seeing my father. In one generation, one family had gone from having very little to watching a son get sworn in to serve America in its highest capacity. A true American story. And an Indian American story.

My story is not unique. Immigrant success in America has happened to many generations and many ethnic communities. After all, we are the land of opportunity. What is unique is the rapidity of the rise of the Indian American diaspora. In the following pages, Scott Haas chronicles the stories of remarkable Indian Americans. A community on the rise. And we're only beginning.

Ami Bera, MD
Member of Congress

ACKNOWLEDGEMENTS

Deep and grateful acknowledgements to the following: Shikha Sabharwal and Pooja Dadwal at Fingerprint! Publishing, Ajay Raju, M.R. Rangaswami, Monica Bhide, Anita Gurnani, Peter Berman, Jenny Ruducha, and Prabhdip Singh and Pavit Kaur (*Violet Hill, Forever*). Special shout-out to my inspiring children, Madeline and Nicholas. And a heartfelt thanks to *Times of India* for running the first interviews that led to this book.

INTRODUCTION

Advisors to Presidents, CEOs of international companies, top physicians, stand-up comedians, musicians, film-makers, telegenic chefs, and world-famous professors at Ivy League universities. These are just some of the professions and accomplishments of Indians in America. In a remarkably short period of time, people from all over India have established themselves as a vital presence in American life, transforming themselves and the communities they live in.

Other groups, notably Jewish, Korean, and Chinese, have well-established histories of extreme and disproportionate success in the United States. But the key and fascinating differences between these immigrants and those from India are the astonishingly short period of time in which Indians have succeeded, and the range of professions in which Indians now have leadership positions.

No other immigrant group has the record of achievement comparable to that of India. It may seem mysterious or somehow related to innate, genetic causes, but the success of Indians in America is, as a matter of fact, due to specific realities and psychological factors. Indians aren't smarter or better than anyone else, so what accounts for the rapid rise in American life in all spheres, from the political to the cultural, from the academic to the world of business?

Of course, it wasn't always this way. While Indians came to North America as far back as the middle of the nineteenth century, it was only in the past fifty years that inroads were made in positions of authority. Prior to that, Indians were, yes, naturally, a part of American life, but there was not a broad sense of a national community or a belief in being able to lead existing American institutions.

That began to change when large numbers of immigrants from India started to arrive in 1965. Up until then, immigration to the United States was restricted by legal quotas established in 1924 that favoured white, Christian northern Europeans. During the period of the Civil Rights movement, however, the federal government recognized that discrimination, based on perceived racial differences, ran counter to efforts to create a society in which access to power was merit based. Ironically, the Civil Rights movement in the U.S., led by Martin Luther King, Jr., was inspired by the work, idealism, courage, and philosophy of Mahatma Gandhi. So it's fair to say that Gandhi had an invisible hand in helping Indians come to these shores!

In 1965, the U.S. Congress established the Immigration Reform Act, which abolished quotas that had limited Asians from immigrating. Prior to the passage of this legislation, fewer than 10,000 Indians lived in the United States.

Nowadays?

Now, India is the third largest source of immigrants to the U.S., after Mexico and China. In 2010 alone, 69,000 Indians moved to the United States. That same year, the estimate of Indians in the U.S. was 1.6 million people. Today the figure is just over three million.

This is the context for the greatest phenomenon of immigration in world history. It is not just the numbers, but the extraordinary success of Indians who have immigrated to the United States that is so amazing.

This book takes the unique, historical, and anecdotal stories of Indians in the United States and explores from individual narratives what helps to account for the achievement.

How did an incredibly diverse group of people achieve so much in so short a time? What do people who are successful have in common? Which different circumstances led to success? Who are the personalities that stand out?

Through an ongoing series of interviews in *Times of India*, I developed a clear understanding of the cultural implications of resiliencies and established goals. Each person I have spoken to has shared a collection of intimate insights into the ways in which their private reckonings have underpinnings in how they were brought up in India or by Indian parents in the United States. Whether it is family, luck, confidence, brilliance, or perseverance—or some combination of these attributes—each individual adds an enormous amount to our understanding of how it is possible for Indians to add so much depth and richness to American life.

As a clinical psychologist, I recognize that the stories I am being told illuminate themes of Indian society. While I can embrace the abstraction of sociology, philosophy, and political theory that led to the massive upheaval of immigration, I am as deeply charmed and fascinated by the particulars of ordinary people who, through their deeds, become extraordinary.

By investing emotionally and intellectually in the lives of the people in this book, we will learn about the broad as well as the specific currents of India. We will also be able to identify in ourselves the habits that lead to success.

One of the most fascinating aspects of immigration, and one which was behind the 1965 Immigration Reform Act, was the implicit moral belief that character transcends race. This book will show readers the characters who transformed both their own places of origin, by leaving, as well as their new homes. By contributing towards the creation of a more egalitarian society through their mere presence, they introduced a new brand of democracy to the culture that enabled them to head West.

And what is as exciting and even more remarkable is that the story of Indian immigration is evolving. People came to India after 1965 due to Civil Rights legislation. More people arrived to get away from the political turmoil of the 1980s in India. With deregulation and economic change in the 1990s, Indians made their way to the U.S. to try out new ideas of entrepreneurship. Education has always been a draw, and in this new century, Indians arrive in the U.S. not just for medical school or to get an M.B.A., but as undergraduates at the best universities and colleges in the country.

With each new wave, the infrastructure of Indian communities, their assimilation, and the modern take of the cultures of their homes, are renewed and changed. The sheer excitement foments vitality that would otherwise be absent. It is a reciprocal relationship at this point in time—Indians change, and Americans change, through day-to-day contact with one another.

These changes are dramatic, subtle, and deeply psychological—with them U.S. society as a whole is influenced. By examining the lives of immigrants, we learn not only about their passions, but we also discover the qualities that make for leadership and social momentum. Immigrants keep societies from stagnating.

These chapters are organized thematically: stories are not grouped together by race, class, caste, age, gender, or occupation. In life, we have opportunities to connect to people, fall in love, work together, build alliances, and plan for tomorrow based on shared ideas and emotions. There are the common themes in each section of this book, and as you read each story, see if you can find them. See what resonates for you and your family.

These personal stories have inspiring threads that can be woven together. As families in India plan and prepare to send loved ones to the States—sons and daughters, brothers and sisters—it's critical to have a close look at and deep understanding of what it is that's going on here. Through appreciation of the success and adversity of previous arrivals, *and those who were born here to immigrant parents*, families will be inspired as well as be able to anticipate the exciting changes about to happen. And who knows, maybe the next chapters written about the progress of Indians in America will be about *your* sons and daughters, and *your* brothers and sisters!

WHERE
WE MEET
A FAMOUS
FILM-MAKER,
A ROCKET
SCIENTIST,
CHEFS, A
HARVARD
ECONOMIST,
WRITERS, A
VISIONARY,
AND A STAND-
UP COMEDIAN

MADE IN INDIA
Vaishali Sinha

Vaishali Sinha is an artist. Which means, in the art form she has chosen, that the films she makes are unflinching, honest, and inspiring in their depictions of the lives of Indians. Not as they want to be seen nor hope to be seen, but simply as they are. It's the kind of moviemaking that changes both audiences and subjects. Not so much forcing people to confront realities or truth that has been buried, but instead a compassionate series of narrative portraits that help others to experience their lives with newfound openness and, ultimately, acceptance.

In *Red Roses*, Vaishali showed women from India who came to the U.S. through marriage and 'family obligations.' What is it like to be uprooted not by choice, but because it is expected of you? How does gender affect one's independence?

Choose Life? was an even franker film: "A short narrative about abortion and personal choice."

Vaishali then began work on *Kashmir*. This movie, which she co-directed, examined the lives of students in Kashmir: the dangers they face, their politics, the private lives.

Working with co-director Rebecca Haimowitz, Vaishali continued her vigorous film-making approach to make *Made in India*. This feature-length documentary is a rather brave movie, 'about the human experiences behind the phenomenon of *outsourcing* surrogate mothers to India.' In her description of the work, Vaishali notes that, "The film shows the journey of an infertile American couple, an Indian surrogate, and the reproductive outsourcing business that brings them together."

Not exactly Disney.

All in all, Vaishali has created an oeuvre that is complex, original, and in the thick of pressing, controversial issues of gender, economy, politics, and disparities within families and the world at large. But what differentiates her work from didactic approaches is subtlety and clarity. She remains at heart an artist: not interested in propagandizing or bending people's wills, but rather illuminating lives so that those living them and those looking in can experience something new. Whether tragic or comic, the lives seen in Vaishali's movies are real in a very deep emotional sense.

Page 25: Light testing for her current film *Ask the Sexpert.*
Off camera with subjects for a series of films for Center for Reproductive Rights on healthcare challenges faced by immigrant women in the Rio Grande Valley, Texas.

At the U.S. premiere of her multiple award-winning documentary film *Made in India.*

How did she start this journey? What about her upbringing in Mumbai led her to make these courageous artistic choices and to succeed in realizing her vision? What is her life like these days in the hipster capital of the world, Brooklyn?

"Our family moved all around," Vaishali explains cheerfully. "All over India. My father was in the air force. But around the time I turned thirteen or fourteen, we settled down in Mumbai, and that's where I started schooling and went to college. At the beginning of 2004, I came to the U.S. to study. Actually, I was working with a women's rights group in Mumbai. And I began to think about (creative) media to highlight women's issues." She pauses thoughtfully. "My degree is in physics, however! I have a B.A. in that field of study. But I found myself more and more interested in film, and after a year and a half working at a film production agency in Mumbai, I left to explore film-making. I realized that what I really needed to do was study film."

Vaishali's sister was already in the States becoming a physician. A few years prior, she had come to do a medical residency and then fellowship in Emergency Room Medicine. Vaishali visited her and, as she put it, "One trip convinced me to move here." She adds, "I needed to get out and broaden my horizons."

Focused and convinced she could do it, Vaishali went to the New School based in Manhattan, and completed a one-year programme in film. Her work, even as a neophyte, commanded attention and she won an award for the movie she made for her thesis, which was *Choose Life?*. The movie also attracted the attention of a top film professor who, seeing her performance as a student in his class, suggested she work with him. She was on her way.

No more physics. A new land, a new direction.

But early on, the political matters of the U.S. were confounding for her. What mattered for her back home in India had relevancies in the U.S., of course, but the forms of discourse differed. As did the ways in which people met, socialized, and affiliated.

"At Parties. Bars. 'Are you a Republican or a Democrat?' I didn't understand all that then. But after ten or eleven years . . .!'" she says with a laugh.

Her foreignness must have added to the experience of learning; her unique perspective as an outsider engulfed by a broad and hubristic culture, diverse but also solid in the sense that many Americans have as being the centre of the universe. The obvious isolation may have provided Vaishali with a kind of intellectual and emotional solitude which can be a fine condition for creating art.

"Just learning the craft," she says wistfully. "Exploring film theory. Learning: 'What is it like to be a film-maker?'"

Vaishali had mentors. Richard Wormser, the professor who chose to work with her, was a top-notch documentary film-maker with decades of experience and knowledge. She worked with him for a year and a half through his production company, and must have learned a lot.

"Pretty soon I realized what I really wanted," Vaishali says. "To make my own film. To be independent." Although she had made a film for her thesis, she now had her eye on something longer. Working to support herself as a waitress and hostess in a restaurant, she had the flexibility to pursue her ambition. Though it had to have been very difficult.

"I started to film *Made in India*," she says. She talks passionately about her ground-breaking work. "I was fascinated by the surrogate mothers. In Mumbai. The fact that their bodies had become commodities. And how these women in India didn't look at themselves as victims. So many aspects to the situation: legal, emotional battles. What happens when someone makes the choice to be a surrogate mother? The film raises questions and muddles them."

With the film behind her, Vaishali remains restless and eager to continue to defy expectations and break moulds. While her previous movies are more overtly about troubled lives due to economic, gender, and political circumstances, her new project is a step in a somewhat different mode.

"I'm now working on a film about Dr. Mahinder Watsa, a ninety-year-old sex advice columnist in Mumbai," she says. "He's old school Bombay, a real gentleman: hilarious, witty, quiet."

She makes it all sound so easy, going from Mumbai to Manhattan, from physics to film, from controversial feminist movies to a sweet picture about a smart, old gentleman with common sense. And while I admire her resiliency in making these fundamental changes in her life, I can't help but wonder: What was it *really* like? How did it feel day-to-day to show up in America? Coaxing the director from behind the camera and putting the lens of the camera on her for a change.

"When I arrived in the U.S., coming from Mumbai, which is very densely populated, I began taking the trains. The subways. Pretty soon I felt more relaxed. I didn't feel guarded. It wasn't a lot of arms and elbows like in India." The uncrowded public space, even in New York City, was a relief. "I let my guard down. I began to forget what it's like not to have someone creep up on me. Not to have someone put a hand on my leg. At least in my experience, it was a huge relief as a woman." She hesitates because the generalization doesn't take into account either the positive experiences in public space in India or the negative ones in the U.S. "I think that honestly it's complicated," she says. "In the context of street harassment, yes, I've been less frequently harassed here, but I've faced aggressive harassment here as well. The two incidents that come to mind happened near parks— Bryant Park and Union Square. In the first instance, I reported it to white cops sitting in a van who never stepped out or took me seriously because I wasn't in need of ER care. In fact, they said, 'This is New York. Get used to it.' In the second instance, passers-by walked right by and nobody responded even though for the first time in my life, I screamed, 'Help!' I was able to push the man off me—he was drunk." She waits a moment so that what she has said might be absorbed. "So in a nutshell I would say that my *initial* experience was a tremendous sense of relief during travel via public transportation mostly because I wasn't fighting off a number of men who might walk by me and harass me physically. But in the subsequent years, I've faced a few incidents of harassment in public space in New York accompanied by a disappointing lack of reaction by police and public. And that carried its own sense of shock in thinking that I expected better from law and order here."

The expectation that the United States should live up to its ideals is something many Indians speak about in conversation with me. What's fascinating and exciting about that, and especially encouraging, is the strong sense of hope people have that the U.S. can indeed protect its citizens and inculcate democratic ideals more fully. This new generation of immigrants is not yet cynical. And the faith that they have in constitutional rights gives much needed vigour to a country with a long history of violent injustice towards people of colour and women.

Still, what were other obstacles facing her? What might people learn from Vaishali in plotting their move to the U.S.? Anticipating struggles ought to help prepare for their eventuality.

"I was lucky," Vaishali is quick to say. "My sister supported me economically. She was practically like my mom. So the whole journey was very exciting—everything was new and fun." That despite a long-distance relationship with a boyfriend in India. And what was it like being seen as, 'an Indian,' rather than a human being?

"It was all great, but there came a point when I got tired of hearing, 'Why is your English so good?'" Vaishali admits. "I felt like a novelty at times. But now it's better. I'm married now to a partner who sees me as a person, not just Indian. My husband is also an artist, a musical director on Broadway. And we have a one-year-old boy, Luca!"

I wonder what advice she has for others who will come from India to the States. Her positive outlook can't be bottled. Her sense of obstacles makes adversity appear to be minimal. But on a pragmatic basis, what can others learn from this exceptional person who makes art that changes our lives?

"I would say that being open-minded is key," she says. "Experience a new culture and remember that you are moving to a new place. I didn't always want to be surrounded by my own sub-culture all the time."

The importance of assimilation is central to what other Indian immigrants have said to me. It's not giving up one's culture, but adding to it.

"Don't come with preconceived notions," Vaishali adds. "Do your research on what to expect, and don't put a label on things."

It's thrilling to have Vaishali in the U.S. She adds so much to the culture. Her freedom as a person and artist is evident in her work. Would she have blossomed had she remained in India?

"There were opportunities here that I didn't have at home," she says. "I'd never have gotten the same start. I could explore my mind. And it has been great to be free of class issues—I wouldn't have worked in restaurants in India! There is no stigma attached to small labour work in the U.S. This country also lets you explore liberal arts."

With both of their accomplished daughters in the States, how has it been for Vaishali's parents? Surely they take pride in their children, but what about the distance between them? Physical, intellectual, emotional.

"My parents never said no," Vaishali says. So the daughters are the product of the belief her mother and father have in her.

"And these days I see my parents a number of times during their annual visit to the U.S. to see my sister and me. I also travel to India every year."

Regrets?

"Things have changed in India in the last five years," Vaishali says. "But when I moved away, it wasn't like that. I got my start here. I wouldn't have in India."

ROCKET SCIENCE
Priya Natarajan

You may not know the name Priya Natarajan now, but remember that you heard it here first. Don't be surprised, then, if one day you see before her name these three words: Nobel Prize Winner.

I'm inside Priya's artfully decorated corner apartment, just outside of Harvard Square, in Cambridge, Massachusetts, and although we have never met before, I feel immediately at home. Unusually for a physicist who delves in abstract concepts about the universe, Priya is very down to earth. Not just modest, but welcoming.

"My family comes from Coimbatore, which is in the foothills of the Nilgiri Mountains," Priya explains. "We are Tamil Brahmins or Tam Brahms. And you'll see many of us in academia."

Priya then mentions what she calls a diaspora of Brahmins from the region. As she speaks, I think of the region's loss of talent and how it meant that the world benefitted from that exile.

"An anti-Brahmin climate took hold in the 1950s and 1960s," she says. "It was the result of a long history of Brahmins exploiting the other castes. So it was understandable and possibly inevitable in that sense. My family was academic. One of my grandfathers was a well-known lawyer. My other grandfather was a lecturer of English—the first 'brown' one, a job he quit as a nationalist to become headmaster of a rural school, which is where he instituted reforms. And my grandmother! She was a physician!"

Priya speaks with pride and knowledge of the idealism that was inculcated in her not just first-hand, but through the family's history of valuing education far more than personal wealth. She heard from an early age that university life was fundamental to her family's identity, for women as well as for men.

"My parents moved to Delhi as part of that diaspora, they are sophisticated, cultured, and cosmopolitan with international connections. And as part of the drive to acquire the best education possible for us, their kids, they encouraged us to explore and find our passion. Success was never about making money."

Priya came to the United States as an undergraduate. It was 1986 and the university was the extremely prestigious Massachusetts Institute of Technology (M.I.T.). She was of sufficient interest to the school to be granted a full scholarship, which was very fortunate since she would not have been able to attend otherwise.

"When I came to the U.S.," she says, "the law was that I could only take $500 out of India. Nowadays many Indians of course pay their way, and there are lots of undergraduate students, but when I arrived, it was unusual to come right after high school. "

Priya speaks with enthusiasm about those early years as a young college student far from home. She describes herself as 'very young' at the time, intellectually curious, and as she describes the way in which she devoured books, her passion for learning is obvious. I know from what she has told me that education was valued in her home while growing up, but I wonder how as a young woman she had the emotional and social confidence needed to develop independently of her family and so far from home in a new country.

"I come from a non-traditional family," she explains. "I had two brothers I left back in India. They didn't want to leave. They became entrepreneurs. I was the only daughter. And I had intellectual interests that were clear to my parents."

Priya, from an early age, stood out. She was interested in everything—history, writing, philosophy, and math. But it was science where she was really gifted. While still in high school she began work on a research project studying sunspots.

"It was unheard of," she says proudly.

The work was inspired not just by her family, but also by a woman from Cal Tech, Dr. Nirupama Raghavan, who had returned to become the director of the Nehru Planetarium, whom Priya calls her first role model. She was hooked by the research and results. Returning from one of his regular academic trips abroad, her father bought her a Commodore 64 to play with and work on.

"I had a computer before any other kids that I knew did—it was new in India," she says with a laugh.

The research yielded a night sky chart for Delhi for use throughout the year. She went on to write programs that could be used to generate the sky at night in any city in the world.

Within a month, her work was used to publish the monthly sky chart in the newspaper. This was still while in high school.

No wonder M.I.T. took her.

"Going to M.I.T. was the best decision I ever made," she says.

Of course, for a person with an appetite for learning like Priya, further education was in her future. After graduating from M.I.T., she went on to Cambridge University in the U.K. and got her doctorate in theoretical astrophysics. She was trained there by the one of the greatest living cosmologists, Lord Martin Rees. It helped to have talent and it helped to have focus.

"I knew I was going to be a physicist from a young age," she says. The more immersed she became in the deepest recesses of science, the more Priya challenged herself. She was never content to accept the status quo. And although so much of what she talks about as she describes her work requires a degree in science in order to be understood fully, Priya manages to explain her work on black holes and mapping dark matter in simple terms. "Along with the thrill of working at the frontier of science I also have a deep desire to understand how science works, and how we create knowledge," she shares. "I am deeply interested in how radical ideas get accepted in science."

She seeks clarity. She wants to understand things at great depth. Seeing that I am interested in her work, but befuddled as well, she tries harder to help me understand.

"I work on black holes—how they form and grow in the universe," she continues. "They are very enigmatic." So enigmatic, in fact, that although Priya goes into great detail over the next forty-five minutes about what it is she is doing, I can't keep up with her. I start by asking one question after another, but I can see that I'm slowing her down with all my inquiries so, finally, I just stop and let her talk.

"I totally love what I do," she says with finality.

Priya's achievements garnered the attention of her peers and in 2000 she was made a faculty member at Yale University. A brief, difficult marriage made for what she calls 'personal drama,' but before long, Priya was back on track. She is now a tenured full Professor.

"There's kind of a mythology in U.S. colleges and universities about meritocracy," she says, "and somehow Indians fit right into that. But let's face it: I am part of the privileged Indian intellectual elite and extremely grateful for the opportunities."

What Priya means is that she entered each of the famous institutions where she studied and taught with a conviction fostered by her family that she was intellectually capable. She had a clear advantage over others who had insecurities, and who felt as if they didn't belong. She knew she belonged. Given her background, she felt at home and comfortable in these academic settings.

"At home, in India," she says, "I was always made to feel that I mattered."

The role of intellectual privilege, going back generations, meant that Priya must have felt that she was carrying on a family tradition. It was not just her success, but also a continuation of a legacy. She has enormous talent, a phenomenal work ethic, and great intellectual versatility along with a family background that afforded her comfort in places where, historically, people of colour were excluded. She surmounted that racism. And yet there was another issue that she had to deal with routinely.

"I was the first woman Fellow in astrophysics at Trinity College at Cambridge," she says. "Of any colour. And one of the challenges then, and subsequently, was how to be assertive, but not aggressive. I'm very feminine. I like to dress well, and I wear jewellery."

Being assertive and getting ideas across as a woman can readily be perceived by men as encroachment. It's a sexist notion, not even an idea, but just ballast to reinforce male authority.

"It's the biggest challenge," Priya says, "being soft by nature and to have to hold one's own in a male dominated profession with an aggressive culture."

Expansive in her outlook, eager to share her ideas, and willing to face criticism makes Priya unique. She is not an academic who confines herself to classrooms or universities, but an outgoing, vivacious person who readily accepts the responsibility of putting forward ideas. And having achieved well-deserved recognition within her field for her research, as well as a tenured faculty position at an Ivy League university, she has chosen to let others outside of science learn more about the importance of the world she knows about, but which we all live in lacking so much of her knowledge.

"I have always wanted to also be a public intellectual," she says, "going beyond popularizing to explain how science is practiced and the sheer excitement of the enterprise."

Publishing essays in the ultra-prestigious *New York Review of Books*, the U.S. journal for thinkers, has enabled Priya to put forward her ideas to a much broader audience to those who, while they don't know what she knows about the universe and physics, benefit enormously from learning more from her. It's clear to me over many hours with Priya that she is a person who doesn't hesitate to explore, and who challenges herself and others. She won't stop until she is convinced that she has pushed herself to the limits (and beyond). I understand that her personal character helps to explain her drive, but what else?

"Of course my family background plays an important role," she says. "You have to be respectable and be liked."

Priya's personal efforts to be taken seriously as a woman and her family upbringing create a fascinating juncture for her. Growing up in a household where, from an early age, she was regarded as highly intelligent and then having to face a world in which being a woman was a barrier meant that there was discord. Maybe she anticipated the challenge, maybe not. Either way, she had to accept the fact that as a woman she would face gender discrimination.

"Usually I do not react," she says when I ask her how she handles slights based on being a woman. "I can be tempered." She smiles. "What I realize is, as I get older, that grace is an enormous strength. Sure, vulnerabilities are there, but I am composed and entirely comfortable with who I am."

Priya describes how coming to the U.S. at an early age, being independent and open to new experiences, and having ongoing international experiences helped to build and strengthen her resolve. She still refers back to India as her foundation.

"Because I grew up in India," she says, "I have comfort with people across generations and I have carried this with me. Within my family, as the only daughter, my father helped me to feel that there was nothing I couldn't do. As for my mother, she's amazing! She has a sense of grace, kindness, and thoughtfulness. She's a very strong woman: magnanimous, generous, and enormously sophisticated. You would think she's royalty! She had a career, too, as a sociologist, which she gave up to raise us."

The relationship between Priya and her parents isn't based on the past either. She tells me that she speaks with her mother and father every day, and that they come to visit her regularly.

As we conclude another of our long talks, Priya says, "I'd like to tell you about my current research and something really exciting, a new finding." I tell her that I'm afraid I won't understand, and she appreciates that and tries to keep it simple. "I'm working on two different problems," she shares. "The first has to do with black holes, how they grow and evolve, and lurk in the centre of every galaxy. The second has to do with the bending of light. All matter in the universe bends light. Light coming from distant galaxies gets bent, and we don't see the original shape." She says more than this, much more, and I try to understand as much as possible. It's not easy, but it's certainly worthwhile. There is nothing dull about the mysteries of the universe! That's what happens when you spend time with a real rocket scientist.

THE VISIONARY
Madhavan Rangaswami

Every now and then a person emerges who is not just intelligent and capable of being a leader, but who also has a global vision that tampers with concepts, perceived knowledge, and even borders. Such individuals are often crushed by the details needed to usher in new eras and new ways of thinking, but on rare occasion it happens that the visions they speak of and put into action inspire others to join with them to create systems and cultures that in their stark originality transform the lives of everyone.

"I came to the States in 1976," Madhavan (M.R.) Rangaswami says, "from a traditional Brahmin family in Chennai. We are Tamil Brahmins or Tam Brahms, and I think of us as still being the heart of the community. And how I got to here is somewhat fortuitous."

Another Tamil Brahmin!

Like many others who came to the U.S., it wasn't so much of a plan as it was a set of circumstances that got things rolling. Certainly having desire and curiosity played important roles, but luck was also important.

"My brother was already here," Madhavan explains. "He had gotten his Ph.D. in electrical in the 1950s in the States. He was part of the early generation of Indian immigrants. So I came to visit him and although I did not have a Green Card, my brother said, 'Why not stick around?'"

Prior to his arrival, education was in the foreground for Madhavan, and his level of preparedness was obvious. He had a B.A. in General Accounting from Madras College. He had attended Catholic schools—Don Bosco and Loyola—and had a degree in General Law.

But the future in India was, if not bleak, at least uncertain. It was during the Emergency, when for nearly two years the country was under a virtual lock-down with elections cancelled, widespread censorship, and a programme of forced sterilization in poor communities.

"'Come here,' my brother said."

Madhavan attended Kent State in Ohio where he achieved an M.B.A., but his arrival was, to put it mildly, without fanfare and, as he puts it, 'classic.'

He smiles as he recalls the person he was once. He now lives in California.

"I had $100 in my pocket," he says, "and my brother's friend was supposed to meet me. Of course, he met me, but sometimes I picture myself in New York City and wonder what would have happened had I not been met by anyone."

From NYC to Potsdam, in upstate New York, where his brother was a professor of engineering, and Madhavan was away from urbanity. The big city had no doubt familiar aspects to it—

From left to right: Late Dr. Srinivas Aravamudan (Dean of Humanities at Duke, who coined the word Indiaspora), T.K. Balaji, Managing Director, Lucas-TVS, India (leading auto component manufacturer), and Mr. Rangaswami himself.

Page 47: Kicking off the Indiaspora Forum in 2015.

the great numbers of people, the commotion, the diversity—but in rural America, what surprised the intrepid visitor?

"So many things," he shares, as he thinks back to the mid-seventies. "For example, the plethora of choices in grocery stores, it was just mind blowing. In India I was used to the typical, little shops that had an inventory of perhaps two items. I was also surprised by the sheer amount of food served in restaurants. People wouldn't eat about fifty per cent of what was on their plates. That's not a habit in India, where we take a little bit at a time."

He thought some more of the days when he was new to America.

"The number of T.V. channels," he says. "There were so many. In India there was one channel and the programming was in black and white." He pauses. "And women wearing stockings! I thought they had webbed feet."

He laughs at his naiveté.

"But the biggest surprise was snow," he says. "In Chennai it's something like ninety degrees Fahrenheit year round. When I left Potsdam to attend Kent State in Ohio, that first year was said to be the snowiest winter on record while the year after it was reportedly the coldest."

Adaptation to the huge range of choices, the plentitude, and a climate that forced him indoors rather than in public space where ideas might commingle and have fruition required stamina, and Madhavan had plenty of that. He was always goal directed, focused, and capable of developing long-term personal strategies which enabled him to accept day-to-day realities.

From left to right: Mr. Rangaswami, his wife Krisanthy Desby, and Rep. Dr. Ami Bera (only Indian American in Congress).

From left to right: Akshai Datta (Sr. Legislative Assistant to Rep. Bera), Mr. Rangaswami, Anand Rajaraman (entrepreneur and VC from Silicon Valley), and his wife Kaushie Adiseshan (entrepreneur).

"I got a twelve-month practical training visa to work after graduating from college," he says. "And because there was a boom in Houston, Texas at the time, I went there and got a job in one week for a large, multinational manufacturing company."

With employment established, it was time to dream a little, to give free rein to his ideas. It wasn't that he was unsettled or restless, but rather that he saw possibilities. He did not want to perpetuate the status quo.

"I took a training programme in computers," he says, "and when I had completed it, I thought: What should I do? Do you remember that scene in the movie, *The Graduate*, where Ben, the recent college graduate, is taken aside and given advice on his future by a friend of his parents? That man turns to Ben, and says, 'Plastics.' That's it. Just go into plastics and all your problems will be solved, that's your future. Well, for me it was someone saying to me: Silicon Valley. Go to Silicon Valley."

It was the early 1980s, the dawn of the technological revolution that forever transformed the planet. And Madhavan was there. Not as a witness, but as a capable, innovative participant.

"This was so long ago," he says, "that the idea of having a personal computer in your home was pretty much unheard of. There was no Internet either."

He recalls applying to a dozen companies in Silicon Valley. He was ambitious, but always pragmatic. Not blinded by his vision of a different future, but focused on how to create the organization needed to get there.

"Lo and behold, a company calls and flies me out," he tells. "They hire me to do quality assurance. To test software. And here it is, thirty-two years later and I think back: I was there during the whole creation of a new technology."

It was a time of experimentation and growth, both in software and hardware, and in the development of systems and organizations that fostered new institutions that would, perhaps ironically, lead to enormous personal change. Societies changed, too.

"I worked for Oracle," he says. "I had a desk right outside Larry Ellison's office—he is still the CEO—and I was under his tutelage for four years. I watched the company grow from having assets of a hundred and twenty-five million dollars to one billion. I took another company public. I was part of a time when there was huge wealth creation."

Having achieved what for most people is an unimaginable pinnacle of success, Madhavan decided that in 1996 he was finally in a position to give back. This philosophy of service, of not being interested chiefly in wealth accumulation strictly for the purpose of self-aggrandizement, helped to guide and steady his course. For if one is working not just for oneself and one's family, but rather for the greater good and for communities, it takes some of the pressure off. Because at that point, the person is acting on behalf of an idea, and if there is failure or if there are big obstacles, it is the idea that is at threat and not the individual trying to realize it.

Group picture of all the attendees from the Indiaspora Forum 2015, held at Airlie Resort in Virginia.

"I became an angel investor, so to speak," he says, "and to date I've helped fund forty companies. I've also been a mentor to many Indians and many Indian Americans."

He returned to the theme of mentorship later in our conversation. It is central to his thinking.

In order to further his ideas and create a network in which others could participate and add to development, Madhavan came up with two organizations.

"Nascom is a large entrepreneurship," he shares. "We develop products and ways to fund them. In late 2014, we held a meeting, which I hosted, in Bangalore. Fifteen hundred entrepreneurs from all over India came. I arranged for Silicon Valley executives to come to India to meet some of the people behind Indian start-ups and see if they could be of help to them. It was essentially building a Silicon Valley ecosystem in India."

He doesn't stop there. The plan is to create ways for Indians to break out of the confines of imposed identity, whether through work or class or caste or *whatever*, and instead meet one another to see commonalities. Then to use what people have in common to participate more openly and influentially in public sectors.

"Three years ago I started to get together leaders in the Indian community," he says, "I'd talked a lot to Jewish friends with influence and prominence and I wanted to understand better how that community had achieved so much. Indians are now about three million in the U.S., about one per cent of the population, while Jewish people are six million, about two per cent, but the presence is different in public life between these two communities."

What did he learn from a comparative analysis of these two vibrant communities both of which place enormous value on education?

"What I found surprising," Madhavan shares, "is that we, as Indians, are successful, but we are siloed. The tech guys here in Silicon Valley, they connect with tech guys. Indian doctors talk to other Indian doctors through AAPI (American Association of Physicians of Indian Origin). Indian lawyers connect to other Indian lawyers through SABA (South Asian Bar Association). Tamils talk to Tamils, and so on. But there wasn't an organization that exists to bring people together from disparate backgrounds."

So he created one.

"The siloed thing," Madhavan explains, "meant that we didn't show collective strength. The organization I helped establish, Indiaspora, collects all the leaders and brings people together."

Started in 2012, Indiaspora gathered approximately one hundred people and met in Mohonk, in upstate New York, to brainstorm ideas.

"I thought we should ask one another: 'What do we do well? What don't we do well?' and so on. From our discussions, we came up with three broad goals. One, to increase visibility and influence. We're interested in inspiring other Indian Americans. We would like to see more civil engagement. Two, to advocate and help shape strong U.S.-Indian ties. We want to connect to India. Three, to build bridges between India and U.S. philanthropy. To help Indian start-ups and NGOs."

Madhavan spoke enthusiastically of Prime Minister Modi's visit to New York City in 2014 as an example of the sort of ties he would like to see strengthened.

"I was there with the crowds at Madison Square Garden when the Prime Minister addressed us," he says, "and it was a great moment to see and hear the joy of people screaming and jumping up and down in their seats."

Indiaspora meets annually, and in January 2013 held an India Ball to honour President Obama. A more sedate affair than Madison Square Garden, but equal to it in a public display of community solidarity. And powerful, too, in that a U.S. President met with and was honoured by a large group of well-organized, politically diverse Indian Americans.

Indiaspora has kept a core group, and each year has added names to it. What strengthens it, in part, is the decidedly apolitical nature of its programmes. Having filed as what is called a 501C3, the organization is forbidden by law from lobbying and political action. Madhavan noted that the Ball for President Obama would be held for any President, Democrat or Republican.

As he spoke of his achievements in the private sector and in the public sector, I wondered more and more about how he had done it. What attributes had he grown up with that led to a remarkable life?

"Most Brahmin families," he says, "don't seek material things. My family valued education. So, for example, in my extended family we have many bureaucrats and academics. I'd ask myself, as I became successful in business, 'Why do I need all this?' 'Can you do things that give back rather than accumulate?' My parents and their values instilled that in me."

It's an ironic problem to have, but I wondered how he is able to create value systems for his children. They grew up with phenomenal wealth, if not its trappings at least with knowledge that it is there, and the ethos of Brahmanic teaching was more abstract than it had been for Madhavan.

"I'm helping with my wife to raise our kids to be global citizens," he says. "I have two daughters, one seventeen and one fifteen, and I have exposed them both to the world. They've been to over thirty countries. My oldest daughter has volunteered in schools in India. Both children have seen how people live elsewhere. I told them, too, that they will graduate college without loans, but that after that they will have to find out what they want to do and earn a living at it. They are more global than just Indian."

Part of the impetus behind the globalization of his family comes from the fact that Madhavan married a Greek-American. The upbringing of his daughters is not a reflection of one culture. I wondered how his family in India reacted to that choice.

"I didn't marry an Indian," he says, "and I didn't come back. I'm definitely sure that there was disappointment on their part about all of that. But you know? I think they grew to accept what I accomplished. My success may have been good enough for them."

He spoke without irony.

The significance of the conversation is obvious, and I ask Madhavan to summarize, if he can, what advice he would give to young people in India who although inspired by his achievements and philosophy might nonetheless feel intimidated or perhaps overwhelmed, thinking that they could not possibly reach their own potential.

He leaps at the chance and speaks readily.

"First, get a mentor. Someone who can help teach you about what choices you need to make as you plan your present and future." He laughs, then. "I got one, but I didn't even know I needed one! You need one. One of my daughters now has a mentor, a woman in her thirties who is the CEO of a company. It's enormously helpful. Second, build in giving back into your model. Don't wait until your forties. Think early in your career of service to others. I should have started earlier. Third, never expect *quid pro quo*." He is adamant on that point, the disappointing notion that in doing something the doer expected something back. He sees that as a failure of character. "Finally," he says, "take risks. Indian culture is not a risk-taking culture. There is in India a huge stigma around failure. Take a year off. Work for an NGO. Take a chance."

THE SPICE OF LIFE
Monica Bhide

Leaving home with the belief or even a conviction that you are setting out on a specific path towards a well-defined goal is how you get out the door. But once on the road, and far from the strictures and censorious looks of family, as well as the self-limiting behaviours that unconsciously you might inculcate until they become habits, anything can happen.

About a quarter of a century ago, in 1991, Monica Bhide, already a child of émigrés raising their children in Bahrain, decided to study engineering. And why not? Her father was an engineer, he worked for a prominent Swiss company, and due to his expertise he received the largesse of a fine salary and opportunities to travel the world. He provided his children with a lifestyle in which they saw themselves as entitled to the riches and achievement of the upper class. He made them realize that no ambition was too great, and he demanded that they expect of themselves the hard work needed to realize that.

Engineering was familiar to Monica; something that she was good at readily, and the effort it took to succeed, while hard, was less demanding than choosing to pursue a course of study that would have been new within her family. She worked assiduously. The approval of grades and her father meant a lot to her. But something was missing, which confused her since she had so much more than many others.

"As a child I always wanted to write poetry," Monica says. "I'd dream, and write in my journals, and imagine new ways of seeing the world."

She developed observations that were unique and surprising, even to her, ways of seeing and hearing that sounded different from what she read in newspapers and magazines, different from conversations overheard at the dinner and breakfast tables, different from what she learned in classrooms, or on the street, shops, anywhere, really, except for what she read in books of poetry or novels written many decades before. She lived a romantic life, an imagined one, and the duality of having

Judging the Embassy Chef cooking challenge at Washington, D.C.

Presenting an award to the Leela Hotel in Delhi,
courtesy the Delhi Gourmet Club.

to meet reality, as it was, and the world in which she lived the fullest, that of the imagination, took a toll.

But at least she was successful in the endeavour to become someone who, ironically, was independent of her family by pursuing the goals that her father had helped set for her.

"My father had sat me down," she reminisces, "and said that writing was not a way to make a living."

Her father's pragmatism, rooted in his own experience as an émigré from a land divided by the Partition, whose family's fortunes had been lost due to war and colonialism, inspired *him*. It was what enabled him to get through dark nights and combat fears of failure. He had no one. He had nothing to fall back on.

With the family having been made destitute, land and property and money gone, no hope of help from anyone, Monica's father had had to be extremely practical. The world needed engineers. He would always be able to make a living and support his wife and children. So why not apply that way of thinking to his daughter?

Of course, her experiences and opportunities, her upbringing, were utterly different than his. But it was honestly all he had to offer her. He was a good father.

Pursuing this course, Monica came to the States and got two Masters degrees, one from George Washington University and the other from Lynchburg, and subsequently worked in the corporate offices of Ernst & Young for thirteen years. Nowadays, she lives in the Washington, D.C. area.

"I didn't hate my job," she says, "but I felt something was missing."

So she would drive to work, do her job, excel at it, be dutiful, and hope that her inner life with its bold aspirations might one day find expression. The repressed hopes were kept vague, like a dim light barely flickering, but she held on to them each day. It took vigilance, and it was noticeably a distraction. She wasn't aware, per se, of the connection between her secret life and the ennui and sadness she felt like a twinge. Meanwhile because of the toll of having two lives, she felt a kind of daily stress.

Hope came unexpectedly and sadly.

"I had a friend who fell and hit her head," she says. "Horribly, sadly, she died. It freaked me out. I mean I thought about my life and what I was doing with it. I was thirty-five years old, my parents were proud of me, I was good at what I was doing, but I was very unhappy. I didn't know what I wanted to do. Not exactly. Thoughts were still forming. But I was so upset about my life that I wrote my own obituary. It was a scary time."

Had she been a failure at her job, it might have been easier, strangely enough. But the success she had had made it more complicated. How could she complain about work when she was so good at it? Doubts gnawed at her. Maybe achievement was a privilege and now she was squandering it rather than trying to advance even further within the company. Maybe she was afraid of surpassing others. Maybe accepting unhappiness was part of life, a process of maturation, and the idea of another life, one in which her creativity would dominate, was childish. Maybe it was time to grow up. She went back and forth on this; it was a mental tossing and turning. A lack of resolve and her ability to feel at home with herself diminished day by day.

So she quit.

"I just quit," she says. "I left my job not knowing what I would do next. I felt I had to in order to stay sane."

Luckily, Monica had a spouse who saw in her what she had kept to herself for so long.

"Sameer said to me, 'You're happiest when you're writing,' and it was funny because even though I knew it was true, and that it was in my bones, it felt as if it was a revelation. Right, I'm happiest when I'm writing!"

Throughout her life, Monica had kept journals, written stories and poems, diaries, and so on. Having a published career was always in the back of her mind, but she didn't dare give voice to her dreams and desires.

"Sameer encouraged me," Monica continues. "He has what we both jokingly refer to as, 'a real job,' he's an M.B.A. And although that career path is so different than that of a writer, what the two professions have in common are a need for focus, long-term development, and brutally hard work."

Monica would marvel at the peregrinations involved in writing, the wandering her mind took, and the words on the page. She welcomed the sheer variety of experience not just needed to write, but also the opportunity to open herself up to the world: to take things in.

"It's taken me ten years," she says, "to be called a writer. To call myself a writer. To say: I write! No one showed me. I just realized at some point that this is what I do."

Monica makes it sound easy, in retrospect, as if she cast off bonds made out of paper holding her back, as if the struggle

was more of a bad cold than a crisis. It's not only the satisfaction that comes from her notoriety on a national level in the U.S. as a published food writer that colours her memory. Her husband, even if she had not achieved a modicum of fame, had a lot to do with her ability to become a new person after a decade or more slogging through the corporate world.

"My husband gave me unwavering support from the beginning," she says. "He's like my coach. I'll get short inspirational emails from him, like, 'What will you do if you don't write?' He helps me maintain my commitment."

So much of what Monica has said to me is highly personal, and it's as if she trounces over her cultural background, as if being Indian had little to do with the initial path she chose of being an engineer or her decision to strike out on her own. It isn't until late in one of our conversations that she talks candidly and in depth about what it means to her to have been brought up by parents from India. Which is at the heart of her story.

"When my father was an immigrant, having left India for Bahrain, he had a special understanding of money," she tells. "He understood its value, and how hard he needed to work for it. That played a role in how I was taught about my initial career: to earn a living was very important, not to depend on others. He treated me the same way, I think, he would have treated a son."

Being a daughter was also a highly significant matter. Monica's generation—she is now in her mid-forties—was among the very first to hold vast numbers of women who saw no reason not to realize their potential *outside of the home*. This vision was supported, remarkably, by her father.

"When my father sent me abroad, to the States, he caught a lot of flak from his family and my mother's family," she says. "But he was very, very confident. He wanted his girl to go abroad to the States! It wasn't easy for the previous generation in either family to accept this. We heard, 'Oh, my God, you are sending your daughter to the U.S.? Are you crazy?'"

So although her father maintained a conservative position, insisting that Monica pursue engineering, he balanced this with unwavering support. He figured that she could do it. He didn't see the writer in her, the dreamer, but that didn't matter. More critical was his advanced notion that not only a young woman could be financially independent, but that she *should* be. Why depend on men?

"Yes, look, in India it's nice to do Arts, was how the reasoning went, but it's not a way to earn a living," she says.

"And yet . . . when I decided, finally, to quit my job I thought enough of my father's authority to ask his blessing. My American friends said, 'Why are you doing that?'. They couldn't understand how important it is in an Indian family to have one's father's blessing for an important life decision."

So what happened?

"He listened patiently," Monica says. "And then he said: 'It's time.'"

That's it? It's time?

"It's time," she repeats. "Because he understood. He understood that it was something I needed to do, and something I would succeed at doing."

Monica's father had a hand in her love for literature. She recalled how he had always read to her when she was a child, from *Little Women* by Louisa May Alcott to Oscar Wilde.

"He emphasized learning and education," she says, "and I think that's a very Indian thing, part of the culture."

Now what you do with that knowledge and expertise is another thing. It took convincing on both sides. Monica had to convince herself that she was making a wise decision, and her father had to believe in her. In asking his permission, she had to make the case to him, and in that process it was necessary to formulate her reasons in a cogent manner.

The blessing 'felt huge, really huge' to Monica. Between her husband and father, she had gained authority as if by osmosis. Both men, inspired by traditional loyalty to family, saw in Monica commitment and ability.

It's been a long, eventful journey and now, ten years into her career, Monica can take pride in her two cookbooks, appearances at international food writing seminars, and publications in major U.S. newspapers and magazines. Named by Twitter as one of the top ten food bloggers in the world, she has helped to introduce the depth of foods from India to the West. Her most recent book, *Modern Spice: Inspired Indian Flavors for the Contemporary Kitchen* (Simon and Schuster, 2009), is a modern take on traditional recipes and ingredients. There is no one quite like her.

"When my first cookbook came out (*The Spice is Right*, 2004), my cousin called me from Delhi, she was so excited! Nothing speaks like success. I mean, I had family who were very angry with me when I quit my job, but once I got published—I now have three cookbooks out—people understood."

Her next goal is fiction, and her short stories are beginning to appear in notable publications, including *Singapore Noir*. She also recently published a collection of stories titled *The Devil in Us*.

Monica creates new challenges for herself, and her discontent as an artist has a foundation in the confidence she has in herself, which is distilled from the backing she has from family. She is intellectually restless because she expects more from herself due to that innate belief.

All along it was her husband whose support she could rely upon. Later Monica added her father. Both men saw it as their duty and a feature of their love to be of help to her. That duty or sense of responsibility stemmed from being part of a culture that emphasizes fierce loyalty to family.

"I met my husband when I was much younger," she says. "I was a student in Lynchburg, Virginia. We were two of the three Indians on campus. It was that long ago. He immediately had confidence in me."

Monica's husband is a mix of the past and the future, which of course pleases her enormously. She is in the 'new world,' but has not ended her allegiance to the valued customs to India.

"Sameer called my father to ask my hand in marriage," Monica says.

And he was given paternal consent.

Monica's passion for writing, a husband who 'coached' her towards achievement, and a father who although pragmatic always came through for her in a pinch. To what else does Monica attribute her phenomenal success?

The other thing was education.

"The competition in India is intense," she says. "My GPA after high school was in the 98th percentile, and the only subjects available to me in the high-end Indian universities were coal mining engineering or English honours! Neither was family approved. So I enrolled in India—in a much smaller school—for a degree in Computer Science. I came to the States after that to study for my masters."

She continues: "My family, perhaps because they are Indian, valued education. Education meant knowledge. They had lost everything in the Partition, and it was from books that they kept growing."

And it is with books that Monica continues that journey, and honours her legacy.

THE BONG MOM
Sandeepa Datta Mukherjee ___

"I hadn't anticipated all the drug-referenced emails to my site, *Bong Mom's Cookbook*," says Sandeepa Datta Mukherjee with a knowing laugh. "But then a friend explained it to me. 'Sandeepa,' she said, 'a bong is something people use to smoke marijuana!' I was so naïve."

Sandeepa was telling me about the start of her blog and the book subsequent to it: *Bong Mom's Cookbook: Stories from a Bengali Mother's Kitchen.* 'Bong' is slang for a person from Bengal, the region Sandeepa comes from, and she had used the word to identify herself. The misunderstanding still amuses her. That she hasn't changed the name of the site or the title of her book, a collection of recipes and memoirs, is an indication of her steadfastness and independence. She was willing to change and adapt to new circumstances in the United States, but she was still going to be a bong mom.

"I came to the United States about thirteen or fourteen years ago," she says, "and all the while we've been here in Marlboro, New Jersey."

It's a small town of just under forty thousand inhabitants, near Edison, the place where many Indians have made their homes, and en route to the Jersey shore.

"I'm from West Bengal," Sandeepa continues, "but I grew up in lots of places: Kolkata, Mumbai, Bangalore. And smaller towns, too, in Bengal. So I've always been accustomed to moving around. The transition to New Jersey was easier in that way."

Not that moving to New Jersey was a plan, nor a decision she and her husband were eager about making. It came about simply because both Sandeepa and her husband are engineers who were transferred there by Siemens, the corporation which employed them. The original idea was to remain in U.S. for three years and then go back to India, but that's not what happened.

"We liked it here," confesses Sandeepa.

The couple made a home for themselves and now have two children, both daughters, ages eleven and seven. The reasons for the family's decision to remain in the States are very specific, which isn't surprising given that both parents are engineers used to thinking things through in a real nuts-and-bolts way.

"It is a wonderful place for our daughters," says Sandeepa. "The environment, for one thing, where there is so little pollution. The overall cleanliness. And the fact that we can have a relatively big home with lots of greenery—that wouldn't necessarily be affordable in the big cities in India."

The suburban life suited the family well. Less to worry about: clean air, clean streets, a private space to call their own with nature encroaching. These experiences pleasantly freed their thoughts.

"We also love the discipline and orderliness of everything in the States," Sandeepa says. "The efficiency is very appealing. Though I do miss the chaos and people back home!"

Sandeepa's enthusiasm is considerable, and as she speaks about what she loved about raising a young family in New Jersey, the list grows.

"Education," she says. "Education is excellent in India but good schools are not affordable for everyone these days, and public school education in India is not that great. There's a very good public school system where we live and everyone is entitled to a quality education."

Which is an enormous relief to her and her husband as they face the challenge of educating their daughters. The partnership that Sandeepa has with her husband helps them both to sort through the complications of wanting to preserve the heritage of their culture for their children while accepting and even encouraging them to enter the U.S. mainstream. The transformation from tradition to modernity requires a great deal of focus and discussion.

"I met my husband sixteen years ago, in Delhi," Sandeepa says. "We were classmates, in the same college, and we were friends; it wasn't romantic." She smiles. "Eventually, it turned into something more."

The young couple decided to marry after they started working. Their careers had parallels, from Mumbai to Bangalore, and marriage was a practical consideration. It was a relationship built on love between Sandeepa and her husband, rather than an arranged match by their families, which of course faced analysis by Sandeepa's family.

"They had their reservations in the beginning," she says, "but eventually my mother came around, and before long she made my father understand."

Sandeepa explains that her parents visit every year, and enjoy the contrasts between their home and the one their daughter and her husband have made for themselves in New Jersey. I asked what, in addition to that which pleases her parents, surprises them.

"When I go with my father to Costco, the huge discount store where people often buy in bulk, he cannot believe the amount of things that people buy. He'll say, 'Why do they need so many kitchen towels? Why do people eat so much?' He thinks folks here are more wasteful."

These questions occur to many Americans, especially the affluent ones, but the sophistication about excess has a different nuance when expressed in similar words from a man who lives abroad. His context is India where in most homes excess is frowned upon or impossible.

"My mother says that she likes it here because there's not so much dust," Sandeepa says. "Back home she complains about the dust in her home."

Encouraged by her parents, husband, and daughters, and living in an environment where she enjoys the natural surroundings and efficient infrastructure, Sandeepa felt free to add other activities to her day-to-day responsibilities as an IT engineer.

"I love the balance between engineering and writing," she says. "It's working."

How an engineer went from science to a life of imagination, and one in which food is narrative and culture, intrigued me.

"I started writing as a hobby," Sandeepa says, "around 2006 or 2007. It all started as a blog. And it wasn't just a cookbook. It was more about my experience cooking, an effort both to be humorous as well as tell stories. I was originally going to write something technical."

The blog, which indeed combines strong narrative with recipes, caught on. Sandeepa soon received a letter from an editor at Harper Publishing in which she was asked if she wanted to write a book based on the blog. The idea was to tell stories using food as a vehicle. It was an exciting, even thrilling invitation.

"That's what I wanted, too," Sandeepa says.

The book came out in 2013, and attracted a wide readership fascinated by the mix of food and culture. The balancing act of being an engineer and a creative artist created a literary tension that is successful. I wondered what Sandeepa is working on nowadays, but she was circumspect.

"I have an idea," she says, "but it's nowhere near completed. I want to do something with fiction."

For now it's writing about food which inspires her.

"As I said, I grew up in several places," says Sandeepa. "Different languages, different cultures, so much variety it made me adaptable. It's what I was telling you about earlier: when I moved here, it was as if it was one more city in India. But what I had experienced from the moving in India was this: every region is different, of course, with its own foods and culture, even if it is within the same country."

Inculcated in her from the journeys was an ongoing appreciation for the depth and authenticity of each region. So that while her writing is about Bengali cuisine, Sandeepa says that she loves everything, from South Indian food, to even Thai and Italian."

One major effect of being peripatetic is that it has made Sandeepa more global in her thinking about food. Not just Indian. She put it this way: "I'm more flexible and adaptable."

At home in at least two cultures, to say nothing of her comfort in several Indian regions that differ in festivals and food, I wondered how Sandeepa's daughters fare when they return to India.

"The most recent time we were in India, we took our daughters during the Durga Puja festival," Sandeepa says. "It was the high point for our oldest daughter, she'd never seen anything like that. Ten to twelve foot high idols. Very opulent and gorgeous. They were very amazed. And the vibrant colours and sounds. The one drawback was that I don't think my eldest daughter liked the crowds so much, and the fact that I wouldn't let her eat *street food.*"

And how does Sandeepa keep tradition alive for her children when they are stateside?

"My younger daughter is learning classical Indian dancing," she says. "Both children are learning Bengali singing inspired by the poetry of Tagore. And although we are not especially religious, we celebrate the Bengali festivals. We also make new traditions I guess as we dole out candies on Halloween and cook turkey with Indian spices on Thanksgiving."

More broadly, and Halloween aside, which has nothing to do with Indian culture, what values do Sandeepa and her husband instil in their daughters which derive from their having grown up in India?

"Honesty," says Sandeepa. "Respect for elders. Education. Importance of family—until I was in fifth grade, our family, like many in India, included in our house cousins, uncles, aunts, and grandparents. We also want our children to understand that life is not always plentiful, and that you must not take things for granted. Basically, it is the same values irrespective of country or continent."

A HARVARD ECONOMIST
Raj Chetty

Raj Chetty's corner office in the Littauer Building on the campus of Harvard University has in it one wall that is lined with books and two enormous windows facing in the direction of Harvard Square and the Cambridge Common. When we meet there, I'm nearly overwhelmed in advance by his reputation. He was the recipient of a 'Genius Grant' from the MacArthur Foundation and is one of the youngest people in the history of Harvard to have a tenured professorship. Raj is only thirty-six years old, and his future is extremely bright.

H is work appears on the front pages of *The New York Times*. He has been asked to consult with President Obama and Presidential aspirants Hilary Clinton and Jeb Bush. His research on economic disparities and the public sector possesses deep originality. In 2008, *The Economist* listed him as one of the top eight economists in the world. And in 2015, Raj was awarded the Padma Shri, for distinguished service in any field, by the Government of India.

So I walk in head slightly bowed, hoping that our conversation will be manageable.

It turns out that I had nothing to worry about.

Raj, thin and of medium height, looking as young and fervent as a graduate student, has on a simple, button-down shirt, ordinary eyeglasses, and his demeanour is humble and welcoming.

I ask him about his past, his history, and I hear a remarkable story.

"I came to the United States with my parents when I was nine," he says. "From Delhi. But my parents were originally from the south near Chennai. My mother was a medical doctor and my father had a Ph.D. in statistics."

What had happened, what had brought them to the States was this: Raj's father was an advisor to Indira Gandhi. It was the period of deregulation in the India economy, a time when the state was transitioning from the control and governmental ownership that was part and parcel of the Nehru era. Raj's father had become an advisor to the Prime Minister, and in

1987 with all that was going on in India, the turmoil, he headed to the States.

After a stint in Maryland, the family found themselves in Milwaukee, Wisconsin, where Raj then grew up. His sisters, being ten years older than him, were already in college and medical school.

"It was a very academic household," Raj explains, "and I knew from an early age that I wanted to go into research. I liked lab in high school, but I also liked abstract work in economics."

According to the Federal Reserve Bank website, Raj wrote an essay while still in high school that 'questioned assumptions and conclusions in *Time on the Cross* by Robert Fogel, a Nobel laureate in economics.' Subsequently, 'as a Harvard freshman, he sent it to the eminent economist Martin Feldstein, asking to be his research assistant. Impressed, and though he rarely picked freshmen, Feldstein gave Chetty the position. Chetty excelled in economics, graduating summa cum laude in three years and completing his Ph.D. in another three. He taught at Berkeley from 2003 to 2009; then he returned to Harvard.'

I understand how growing up in an academic household with two highly educated parents can lead to achievement, but I'm left wondering about the direction of his work. His thinking has remarkable strains of empathy. His work examines economic disparities, and questions what amounts to a broad societal indifference to or acceptance of poverty and its consequences. How is it that Raj came to care so much about the poor that his career as an economist focused on their conditions? Where did his empathy come from?

"The India my parents left was more liberalized under Prime Minister Gandhi," he says. "There were changing issues and it was definitely inspiring. Another thing: my mother's grandfather. He was a freedom fighter who worked with Mahatma Gandhi."

Not just that. It was not just a culture of liberalization or a great-grandfather who fought for India's political and economic independence. Within his own house there was a climate of possibility and open-mindedness.

"My mother was the first woman in our community— Chettiar—to become a physician," he says. "Her father invested in her. The family was poor, and like many poor families in the 1950s, it was clear to them that not all of their children could get higher education. They had to choose. She had five or six siblings. Her father chose her."

Growing up with a mother who knew that she had been chosen to succeed, with the burden and thrill of that powerful and confident investment based on preference, meant, too, that it was a house in which sacrifice was well understood. Education came at a price: one child would be granted the largesse that comes from a medical degree, the others would not. Some sense of the authority of education must have been part of the family's philosophy.

"My mother became a paediatrician," Raj says, "and she was always very focused on helping people. Not just patients. She helped bring her whole extended family to the U.S. She always did things for the community, and helped others take advantage of opportunities. So part of my mission, in addition to doing something as rigorous as research, is to try to have a positive impact on the world, and to treat my work not just as a job, but as a way to make a meaningful difference."

Raj's work is thoroughly analytical, deeply creative, and grounded in research methodology that make his results of enormous value to those in positions to create political changes. But what's also unique and remarkable about him is the ways in which he weaves a pragmatic and heartfelt approach into his scientific thinking. His work may be abstract, but it seems that temperamentally Raj is not. That's what makes his research so appealing. It really can make a difference, and that reality stems from embracing his family and culture.

"It is important to increase opportunities for kids of low economic backgrounds both in India and the U.S.," he says. "One example: I recently completed a study of the U.S. Is it a land of opportunity?"

Raj is referencing his landmark new study, quoted as the lead article in *The New York Times* in April 2015, that shows, county by county nationwide, how where a person grows up has enormous consequences on how much he or she will earn as an adult. The answer varies, of course, and if a person comes from a low-income family on the East Coast or the Rust Belt or the Southeast? All of that matters.

From his research, it becomes apparent that growing up poor in places like the Rust Belt or the Southeast of the U.S. lower the odds that a person will be able to overcome the barriers imposed by his or her economic class. In contrast, growing up poor in *some* urban centres on the two coasts is not as confining. (Or it can be worse, as in the case of Baltimore County.) The staggering numerical data turns the discussion of what has long been regarded as a political problem into one that is economic. Raj reframes the crisis and places opinions and emotion alongside statistics that are frankly irrefutable.

"There are key factors," Raj explains patiently. "Education, for example. The quality of teachers from elementary school up." He notes infrastructure as well. "The degree of segregation: with more integration, there is data to show that there is greater overall mobility." Then, too, a finding that I hear from many other Indian Americans, and which seems to be fundamental to success in any community. "Mentorship." People within the community, successful in any number of ways or vocations, who take on the role, informal or not, of teaching the youth how to go about organizing and planning their lives so that one day they can take the reins.

Litigation in the U.S. has led to change in communities. Forced by federal U.S. courts to end discrimination in housing and education, for example, means that opportunities can be created for the poor. One of the most exciting things about this country is that it is restless. Things are not static. Change isn't just possible; it is sought after and embraced. And a huge part of the reason for that mentality is the role of immigrant groups, such as the waves of people from India, who keep stirring the pot. Raj just happens to be pivotal in that mesmerizing process.

He notes his family again as having been a big part of his inspiration to create change. While he is world famous for his work, others he is related to have not had his good fortune. Being aware of the disparities within his own family helps him recognize the role of luck and timing in shaping identity.

"I have a number of cousins named Raj," he says with a laugh. "I'm the Boston Raj. There's a Chennai Raj as well. And I've been lucky. I think that my cousins would have been lucky, too, had they had my opportunities. I have one cousin, for example, who does manual work and has to commute two and half hours every day. Another cousin works in a temple in Singapore. So much is random chance. Seeing people whom I'm close to live different lives, I get a very broad perspective." He pauses thoughtfully. There is an artistic streak I detect in him, an ability to transform his emotions into creative work that is meaningful to others. "I have family around the world. And I know that achievement is not merely the result of hard work. My parents happen to have been chosen by their parents to succeed. My mother's education, for example, being paid for by her parents. My family shapes my outlook."

As he talks about the role of geography in predicting income growth in the U.S., I think about India. Would Raj's models of research apply there as well?

"Yes," he says, "it's not country specific. You have some of the best schools in Asia. Going to them creates opportunity. Or look at the Taj Mahal. Such an incredible contrast between it and the total poverty outside."

Raj speaks again and again of the appreciation he has for his father having come to the U.S. and how that move allowed for an expression of intellectual potential.

"My father first came to the U.S. with my mother to be in a Ph.D. programme before I was born," he says. "And then returned to India where *I* was born. When they returned to the States, this time with me, my father saw an astrologer who told him he had better not go, that the ship would sink." He laughs. "My father said, 'There's no way he knows what he's talking about!'"

So there he was, Raj Chetty, a future world-famous Harvard economist, but at the time a boy from India in an ordinary U.S. elementary school. What was *that* like?

"I was entering the fourth grade," he says wistfully, "and one thing I remember is this: In Indian schools, the students stand as a sign of respect when the teacher comes in the room.

So when I stood up in that American classroom, the other kids made a lot of fun of me."

Then there were the kids who teased him about his accent back then as a new arrival.

But who has the last laugh?

THE NUMBERS ADD UP
Veerappa Chetty _____

After removing my shoes inside the foyer, I follow Veerappa Chetty, who is barefoot, past a large, open kitchen and then into a slightly sunken living room into which light is pouring from outside.

The illumination comes through big bay windows that look out onto a manicured yard surrounded by young deciduous trees, and then from down below, where a deep, spring-fed New England pond lies shimmering. We are in his home in Arlington, which is an economically diverse suburb of Boston, at one time chiefly middle class and now one rung above that in many homes due to the economic boom of the city.

Veerappa, who goes by Chetty, may be best known these days for being the father of Raj Chetty, who is the darling of Harvard's Economics Department, and the author of watershed documents on economic disparity which have caught the attention of President Obama. But he is, in his own right, not only the progenitor, but a man whose modesty at times is at odds with his achievements in the use of statistics in governmental policy. He lived in a different era: when there were few Indians in visible positions of prominence in the United States. And I can't help thinking what his career would have been like in this country had the racism been less obvious and insidious. But even during a time when unmovable barriers existed, Chetty made a name for himself on two continents, and these days continues to be highly regarded in the crucial field of healthcare economics.

As a man whose efforts and sacrifices helped to create the infrastructure that enabled the next generation of Indians to make it in the U.S., what's his story? What lessons might we learn?

"I completed my graduate studies in 1966 in the U.S. with a Ph.D. in Economics," Chetty explains, "and then in 1972 returned to India. For two reasons. I was a full professor here and I felt that there was not much to achieve. Secondly, my wife, who is a paediatrician, was always saying as a complaint: 'I see only coughs and colds whereas in India I'll treat hundreds of very sick children.'"

Chetty quickly found work at the Indian Statistical Institute in Delhi, and his wife began work as a doctor. He

built sophisticated models having to do with monetary policy, and, as a true intellectual, read deeply in a wide array of fields, which he continues to do to this day.

"About a quarter of my time, I'm reading lots of books on psychology," Chetty says, "and I'm fascinated by recent developments in neuropsychology."

Talk about brainy!

Previously, from 1962 to 1972, when he had been living and working in the U.S. before returning to India, Chetty taught Economics. He also consulted to the United Nations where he worked with Manmohan Singh, the future Prime Minister of India. Singh was an economist, too.

Singh returned to India at the same time as Chetty. The two had become friends in the States. Singh contacted him in India and asked him to be a consultant.

"I like to say that I learned economics in India and not quite as much in the U.S.," Chetty says with a laugh. "In India, I helped build fancy economic models using money. Developing monetary policy. Let's say, deciding how much money to print." His ability to simplify extremely complex matters that fill up books speaks to his talents as a professor. He reflects on how that knowledge helped him when working with (future P.M.) Singh. "At the end of one year, I walked into Singh's office and said, 'You paid me Rs. 6,000, which is $100 today. Hereafter I will not accept any money in India for consulting.' And I added: 'One day when I feel confident enough, I'll advise you for a real fee.'"

Chetty set about trying to sort out monetary policies that might help the Indian government under Indira Gandhi, which at the time was decentralizing somewhat as well as creating a private sector from previously State-owned enterprises that had developed under P.M. Nehru.

"Money is so complicated," Chetty says. "So I chose the simplest commodity: sugar. I studied three hundred and three factories. This involved making predictions: 'How much sugar output can be expected one year in advance?' The prediction turned out to be correct and people started coming to me for advice." What next? "Next I studied the steel industry."

Back in India to contribute to the well-being of his home country, Chetty and his wife set about raising their two daughters and son. They were already living in Delhi fifteen years when Raj was born.

"My wife and I were fortunate to bring up our children in Indian culture," Chetty says, "and we also felt that we could provide them with a good education in Delhi."

The children attended elite schools in Delhi, and then there came a point when Chetty and his wife decided to return to the States. But before that decision was made, Raj was showing signs of prowess.

"We applied for Raj to two of the best schools in Delhi," Chetty explains, "and he got into both of them. At one of the schools, parents had to be interviewed along with the child. Raj was five at the time. He was given a psychological test of some kind and when that evaluation was over, and he was led out of the school holding my hand," —Chetty laughs at the memory— "he turned to me and said, 'I passed the test and in case you fail, will the school take me?'"

Education at the higher levels was fine in India, but Raj was a priority due to what seemed to be, early on, prodigious academic skills that might be boosted stateside more thoroughly.

"These were all calculated decisions," Chetty says. "At what age should we make a change? So we consulted educational psychologists, and the consensus was that a good time to start in terms of a transfer of schools would be the first year of middle school. Not the second, but the first." All the students would be at a new point in their schooling. "At each stage, we made decisions. And it was a real change! Such as: in India, when a teacher enters a room, the students are all expected to stand up.

And to speak before being asked a question by the teacher it's considered to be disrespectful. Not in the States."

The family moved to Bethesda, Maryland, outside of Washington, D.C. The school was good, home life was good, but there were problems of acculturation.

"My wife and I started reading books about how to bring up issues with teenagers," Chetty says. "How to talk to them. Our kids were exposed to a different culture and there were at the time very basic differences between our two cultures." Such as? "In India you didn't talk to a girl until you were married to her. Arranged marriages were the norm. Here it was *very* different. Parental involvement is very minimal."

When Raj turned thirteen, the family moved to Milwaukee, Wisconsin, in the Midwest, as Chetty had a job at the university there. Chetty taught and prospered, and continued to help raise a family. Eventually, he moved back East. And now with his years of government service in India and his professorial duties informing his ability to make choices, he turned to a field in need of his numerical expertise.

"In India I had worked on the economics of fixing prices and public policy," he says. "In the U.S., it's different because for the most part it's a totally free economy. So I thought: What's the one area of the U.S. economy where prices are fixed through government policy?" The mere question is brilliant, precise, and analytical. And the answer, as you'll find out, is marvellous, because it is one of the sectors that drains the economy, provokes profound emotional responses, and is a massively confusing mix of private and public monies from all sorts of industries, from medical to corporate to pharmacological to insurance; it's a mess. "The health sector," says Chetty. "Medicare. Look, I'm a statistician. I'm fascinated by the science of errors. If there were no errors, it would be pure mathematics. One of my interests, therefore, was to find some good errors. For example, with Medicare, you have to make a choice to do a medical procedure. Sometimes the outcome, depending on the choice, is 50-50. Sometimes it's 70-30. Both 'errors' are equally costly." Statistical analysis can help measure outcomes and predict, in part, the best allocation of funding. "There is no gold standard in economics. No 'Did you do it right or wrong?' What is the truth? There's no way to find out." I can see why Chetty turns to psychology in his reading. The more he talks about numbers, the more evident it is that human behaviour plays a huge role in statistical outcomes. "And that's what made me so happy with my studies of Medicare. There is a pathology report." We can see what happens if a procedure is followed. Or not followed. "I can know what the truth is."

All the while that Chetty was learning and teaching, he was growing as a person. His love of others existed alongside his passion for numbers, and it is that empathic quality which contributed mightily to his being part of a viable Indian American community in the United States. I can also see where, in part, his son Raj's empathy comes from. Both men believe in the importance of relationships.

"I believe a lot in having very good friends," Chetty says thoughtfully. "People who have an interest in you and tell you bluntly what they think. About two years ago, in studying

Aristotle, I came across his concepts of three types of friends. There is the utilitarian type: like a farmer whose kids you let play on your land so that he will help you at harvest. There are friends for pure pleasure: like small children who play together day-to-day in school and have no expectations of one another. And then there is the perfect friend. What is a perfect friend? One who thinks about you and tells you what he thinks of what you're doing. Just because you're friends. And doesn't expect anything in return."

Chetty's personality is a unique mix of the intellectual, pragmatic, philosophical, and personal. I think he is a rare sort of person until he tells me, finally, about his ancestry. *He's* still unusual, but then, too, so is his *family* history.

"Chetty is an ancient banking community," he explains. "Going back about one thousand years. Nehru used to say that three communities financed the whole world: Jewish, Chettiars, and Marwaris. The Chettiars are said to have financed East Asia, including Singapore, Malaysia, Burma, and Vietnam."

But for all the money that Chetty understands in a highly intuitive way, he remains at his core a man of principles guided by his love of humanity. He's neither a banker nor a person indifferent to income disparities. On the contrary, over the past two years, he tells me, he has been studying problems highlighted by Thomas Piketty in his monumental work, *Capital.* Chetty is guided by his rather optimistic views of society as being dynamic, and capable of fairness through the spread of knowledge and the use of numbers to understand and build policies. That outpouring of intellect helps the world, and it specifically has contributed to building an infrastructure for Indians in the States.

"I keep in mind some important axioms," Chetty concludes. "First, everyone wants to be happy. Second, no one therefore knowingly does anything to hurt himself or others. And, finally, it is lack of knowledge that leads to unhappiness."

It all adds up.

STAND-UP COMEDIAN
Vijai Nathan

Engineers, doctors, IT specialists, professors, business people, lawyers, politicians, publishers, novelists, and poets. The Indian American community is nothing if not diverse and accomplished, ready to take on new challenges and invent solutions where others were stymied or blocked. In the initial large waves of immigrants, which followed changes in federal U.S. laws, Indians coming to the States were pursuing higher levels of education, which often led to traditional and highly remunerative professional lives. Ironically, the huge and unprecedented success of these previous generations created a framework which allowed their children and grandchildren to be frankly more imaginative.

It's not an uncommon phenomenon in any number of immigrant groups that came to the U.S., and it leads to misunderstandings, anger, and accusations in both directions. The people who came to the U.S. adopted old school ways of getting things done, worked long hours at jobs they often did not find emotionally or intellectually satisfying, and focused on establishing for themselves and their spouses and children a valid and financially secure place in the U.S. society and their neighbourhoods. The goals were to achieve vocational and social status: to be valued.

It's easy for the children of immigrants born in the U.S. to forget, since it wasn't really part of their personal experience, the struggles which took place for their parents' and grandparents' generations. Besides, truthfully, having heard on and on about the sacrifices made on their behalf, maybe the generation of Indians who self-identify as Americans, may be a little tired of that same old narrative.

That combination of forgetting and fatigue leads young Indians who grew up in the States to come up with new identities utterly separate from those foisted upon them. It's not quite enough to hold onto the past and to become the person your parents fantasized you'd be.

And because that process of becoming comes in fits and starts, without a protocol or set of rules, it can be quite funny. At least for the person who is going through it. Viewed as rebellious at times by their families, even 'black sheep,' the children of immigrants are often intransigent in their conviction that having been given the good fortune of freedom that, well, they ought to

be free. They don't have to fit in; they don't have to be accepted by Americans—they are Americans! And isn't that the purpose of coming to a new country?

"I grew up in Maryland," says Vijai Nathan. She's lived in Montreal, NYC, and LA; these days she's in Washington, D.C. "My parents came here in 1970. My father worked for the World Bank, and was brought here by them. He has both engineering and law degrees. A U.S. law degree and also a U.S. M.B.A. My mother was a homemaker, but she also went to college in India and in the late 1970s, she got an M.S. in library science from the University of the District of Columbia. They left from Chennai."

Vijai's father died in 2007.

"His father, my grandfather, was in the film business," Vijai says. "He owned a movie house, but there was a fire, it went up in flames, and he lost everything."

Her mother has a more illustrious family background.

"My mother is the youngest daughter of Namakkal Kavignar V. Ramalingam Pillai, the poet laureate of the state my family is from," Vijai explains. "His poetry was taught in schools and his books were turned into movies. He is best known for his book *En Kathai* or *My Story*. He was a Gandhian poet. There's even a postage stamp in India with his image on it! He died when I was ten months old. I so wish I could have known him."

Vijai's family background is the context for her experiences as an American. What makes her unique within the family is that of all of her siblings, she is the only one to have been born in the States.

"My two older sisters were born in India," she says. "My oldest sister, who came here when she was eight and a half, is a doctor. My next oldest sister, who came here when she was four and a half, is a lawyer."

The great thing about comedians is that the best ones tell the truth. The laughter that follows their jokes is a relief—tension is dissipated, and what's said is usually not meant to be heard. They approach taboos not with caution, but with mischievous delight. Like her grandfather, the poet who helped to inspire India's freedom fighters, Vijai says what is on her mind without fear of consequences. Knowing this, I ask what it was like to grow up Indian in a southern state known, in part, for its conservatism.

"They hated us in Maryland," Vijai says immediately. "I'd hear, 'Get out of our country, you goddamned foreigner.' Things like that. One summer, I was nineteen, and I got a job as a waitress at a country club. There were a lot of assumptions about me because I am Indian, and a lot of older people who would say, 'You speak such beautiful English.'" She laughs now, but it is doubtful that she laughed then. "I went then to McGill University in Montreal where I studied English literature."

Mixing the past with the present, heritage with contemporary demands and possibilities, was routine. It's normal to assimilate, which in Vijai's case meant reconciling values of her family with growing up here.

"I was the only Indian kid in school," Vijai says. "Because my sisters were older, we weren't in school together." But outside of school, the Tamil community was cohesive and assertive.

"Tamils created a temple in our area. Prior, the closest one was in Pittsburgh, which was a considerable distance away." And yet. "We celebrated Christmas. In our own way." She laughs again at the modification which took place: "The holiday marking the birth of Jesus and his brother Santa Claus!"

There was a lot of back and forth between the two powerful cultures, Indian and American, and the differences, in retrospect, seem to be exciting. Though at the time she first experienced them it must have been jarring.

"Our social lives were always around Indians," Vijai says. "So there I was at Kindergarten, thinking: 'Oh, my God, all these white people!'"

Her sense of humour makes Vijai more alive than many others. It is her way to get a healthy perspective on situations that get others down. Her humour, like poetry, is part of her resiliency.

"From 1971 to 1979, we lived in Gaithersburg, Maryland," she says, "where racism was very overt. Kids wouldn't want to play with me at times. I was called names: 'Blackie.' I was bullied at school. I'd hear, 'Go back to your own country!' Parents wouldn't correct their kids when I was belittled. I ended up with friends who were nerdy or foreign or both. Outcasts. We were not embraced."

At home, support was forthcoming, but with a twist.

"My parents would say to me, 'You are not American, you're Indian,' and 'Don't think you can do whatever you want, you're not free.' They didn't quite believe in American traditions like . . . freedom!" She laughs. "I'd hear: 'You are an Indian.

You need to focus on school. Obey your parents!' Adding to this was the fact that my father's mother came to live with us. She spoke no English. And that's the reason why I speak Tamil as fluently as I do."

But living in an Indian home in the U.S. while attending a school in which being Indian meant something else entirely was conflictual.

"'You have to be Indian. You are not like them.' That's what I would hear at home," Vijai says. "But then at school, my family felt foreign as I thought about them in comparison to what I saw and did there. I was not one or the other." She pauses. "I guess you could say I was ABCD: American Born, Confused Desi. Look, Indians in India don't think I am American. But how do you account for an Indian American identity?"

Vijai's efforts to establish an identity are ongoing, and really very much what makes her the person she is today. Her insight into the fact that these efforts do not constitute a crisis, but are instead a rich fabric of her personality give depth to her comedy. She appreciates contradictions.

After college, Vijai turned to writing and performing comedy not as some facile therapeutic means of trying to resolve conflicts.

"It's a challenge to be a female comedian," Vijai says. "Women comedians, for example, when they talk about sex? It becomes a moral issue. It's a double standard in comedy, a tight rope." Vijai notes other challenges. "I'll be performing in India soon, and I'm hearing, 'Keep it PG.' Only the way they put it is: 'Keep it vegetarian. No non-veg!'" She laughs. "Hey, I can be family friendly!"

But the path to performance wasn't mapped out. It rarely is for entertainers. Adding to the ups and downs of becoming a professional comedian were the expectations of her family. They had wanted her to enter a profession, to be more traditional.

"I wish I was more science-y," Vijai says, "but science is not my strong suit. I knew I'd never be a doctor. I couldn't excel at it. That left what? Majoring in English Literature. Which my father only allowed because he considered it was pre-law."

But after finishing university, not interested in law, meant that Vijai had to come up with an independent plan. One that didn't fit into the family's plans for her, but what?

"I didn't know what to do with my honours degree in English literature," she explains. "I'd studied feminism in Gothic literature. So much Shakespeare. White guy stuff. Anyway . . . I had finished my thesis at college and decided to apply to the London School of Economics. At the same time, I applied for an editorial training programme with a newspaper. So I got into the LSE and I got the job." She pauses. "I took the job."

The time spent training to be a journalist added pragmatism, swift deadlines, and a real audience to her passion for language.

"Becoming an editor helped me become a writer and comedian," Vijai says. She was good at the work. "I ended up at *Newsday*, but it wasn't for me. Then I went to *The Baltimore Sun* for two years. I got engaged, we broke up, I was unhappy about a lot of things. So what happened was this: I took a class in stand-up comedy! As a kid, I always wanted to be a performer. I admired comedians such as Eddie Murphy, Billy Crystal, and Whoopi Goldberg. Anyway, the class was at an adult education school in D.C." She laughs again. "Not the funniest bunch of people. The idea was to learn to be a comedian in two sessions." The idea alone is hilarious. "I decided to do something just for me."

The year was 1996, and the path was becoming clear. The exhilaration of letting it all out must have felt like the cool, fresh air after a storm.

But I wonder what her parents thought. What Vijai was doing was far from what they had imagined for her.

"The first time my mother and father saw me," Vijai says, the words tumbling fast, "it was a long set, something like twenty to thirty minutes. They loved it because they saw how much people were laughing. And my mother," —Vijai laughs, imitating her mom's voice— "'Why are they laughing? You are just saying the conversations from our home!'"

It's not a goal, but through her comedy Vijai demonstrates to her audiences, comprised of all sorts of people, that humour has no borders, that what she finds funny specific to growing up Indian in America has universality.

"I'm going to show that Indian families are just like other American families," Vijai says. "And I don't only speak about my Indian American experience. I talk about racism, but not only. All this took me a few years." It's an ongoing process. "And it wasn't until I came to New York where many people know about Indians, and are around them all the time. My performances became real, it wasn't just an act."

There is no logic to Vijai's trajectory, no explanation for who she became as a person nor comedian, no predictions that came true in terms of her evolution. But in many ways, Vijai is the natural antidote to a world of racism as well as the inevitable progeny of a famous freedom fighting poet and parents who demanded excellence of their daughters.

"A lot of comedians are outsiders," Vijai says, "who want to connect. In many ways, American society's perception that I was foreigner drove me to be a comedian. I wanted to show that my family and I are not so different from any other family in America. *All* parents tell you what to do, mine just happened to have an accent."

THE WRITER
Visi Tilak

I'm meeting with Visi Tilak at Tatte, which is a storefront Israeli bakery in Brookline, Massachusetts with several branches throughout Boston, and although Visi and I have never met before, within minutes I feel as if we've known one another for decades. There's a frankness, warmth, and poise about her, a willingness to engage and share her story with others. She is also a good listener, quick to pick up what an interviewer is keen on knowing about her. But throughout it all, her reserve and confidence are paramount.

"I come from a well-known Brahmin family," she says, between sips of cappuccino. "From Chennai. So the family was Tam Brahm. Another famous Tam Brahm in the region was Srinivasa Ramanujan." I had not heard of him. "Very famous. Math genius. He was the subject of a recent movie, in fact."

Ramanujan was one of the most famous people in her community in that region, but others within her own family were also high achievers. Visi comes from an illustrious background, by any standard, and as I listen to her talk it is evident that she carries on a tradition in which personal excellence, recognizing and living up to potential, might as well be the family motto.

"My paternal grandfather was on the boards of several multinationals and advisor to ministers in the regional government," she says. "And my maternal grandfather was a lawyer who was very involved in the freedom movement which led to Independence; he did a lot of work in that struggle. Further, on both sides of the family, for several generations, there were very highly educated people. Although I will say that my mother *initially* stopped her schooling in the twelfth grade as her father didn't want to send her to college. Meanwhile, however, all five of her brothers completed high levels of education."

Visi, drawing on the family tradition of education, came to the U.S. in 1990 in order to attend Iowa State University in Ames, Iowa, which is America's heartland, far from the big cities and urban sophistication of the coasts. Although her mother had been denied a university degree, Visi was seen by her parents as deserving.

"I was totally spoiled," she says with a laugh. "I got everything I wanted. And it was clear, too, that my parents really wanted me to get an education."

Not attending a university *at first* didn't stop Visi's mother either, and her resilience must have been a big part of her inspiration to take on risks and challenges. When Visi was in elementary school, her mother went onto college where she studied English literature and passed with honours became the number one student in her class.

"My mother then became a journalist," Visi explains. "She wrote for the *Deccan Chronicle*; the Children's section: puzzles, stories, etc. She retired about ten to fifteen years ago." Visi pauses. "That's what got me into journalism."

Having a prominent background, both in community as well as education, and a mother who stood up for herself meant that Visi had role models and social expectations which contributed to her success. It was a broad combination of factors; chief among these was a big family network of brainy achievers who fully expected her to join them.

"Everyone I grew up with had achieved a lot in a range of fields," she says. "Such as science, math, engineering, and medicine." Being intellectual and demonstrating skills to others was the norm. "My first newspaper article was published when I was in the tenth grade. And I continued to write through college."

Visi attended Osmania University in Hyderabad. Being groomed for a medical career, she achieved a B. Sc in Botany, Zoology, and Chemistry, minoring in English Literature and French. While science was a framework for her studies, Visi's love remained for language. As she speaks, describing her life, the natural feeling for words is readily conveyed and it's obvious how studies in language and journalism took place on a bedrock of talent.

"I went on to get an M.A. in English," she says. "This was while I was going to night school to get a Journalism Diploma and working for *The Indian Express*. As a reporter, I covered anything and everything local: politics, art, and culture. I did that for a year."

Challenging herself, and always seeking new ways to improve, Visi did not settle in. The job it seems could have lasted years and years, and it would have been a nice career, but her potential was greater. Fortunately, she had the ambition to match.

"I was recruited to go to Iowa State," she explains, "to study technology and social change through journalism. While there, I got an M.S. in Journalism and Mass Communication. Basically, it was an opportunity to gain expertise in reporting on technological advancement in the developing world. And when I finished, I had as a goal the idea of working perhaps for the United Nations or U.S. AID. But before that might be realized, I did a lot of work for *The Iowa State Daily*, and enjoyed writing more than whatever else I did."

In between developing her métier as a writer, Visi met her husband and started a long-term relationship with him. He was from India, but living in Seattle.

"He was the son of a family friend," she says. "My family wanted me to have an arranged marriage. I know, arranged marriages have a bad rap." But the two had a lot in common. "I grew up in a liberal household," she explains further. "The sky's the limit! And my parents put a lot of trust in me." That trust applied to decision making. Ultimately, the couple made the decision.

Tilak is the first name of Visi's husband. Their families became very close. People within both families felt connected. After marriage, Visi moved to Seattle.

"I decided to try my hand with a Public Relations agency," Visi says. "But after a year I realized: it's not for me. I was asked at one point to promote disposable diapers and to write a press release saying that they do not fill up landfills, which just isn't true. It became an issue of principles."

So after leaving the world of public relations, Visi returned to her love of writing. She became a correspondent for *India Today*. She worked for a publishing company and wrote book and encyclopaedia chapters.

Moving next to Ann Arbor, Michigan, due to her husband's enrolling at the University of Michigan, Visi got more deeply involved in technology writing. This was at a time when the web was just getting started.

"And because my husband had become a student," Visi says, "I became the breadwinner in the family."

After her husband completed his education, getting an M.B.A., job offers were, 'everywhere,' and the young couple chose Boston. Visi started work in marketing for a database company, followed by another role at a streaming media start-up where she was heading up the marketing department and when she became pregnant with her first child, decided to move on.

"It was my last full-time job," she says. "It was very important for me to be there for my children when they were growing up. I don't believe this diminished my intellect or leadership capabilities in any way. In fact it only improved it."

Visi's journey was enhanced by her having grown up with social status and from being raised in an extended family of high achieving intellectuals. But I wonder what barriers stood in the way when she arrived in the U.S. It can't have been easy to be Indian in a rural part of America where most people were white.

"I was in Ames, Iowa in 1991," she says, "and it was the time of the first Gulf war. I used to wear a bindi then, but I stopped. People there assumed I was an Arab." She hesitates. She does not seem to be a negative person by nature. "I got cat calls. I was only one of two Indian women in a class of sixty-five." So what did she do? Did she cave in? "The two of us started wearing our bindis."

Although the pain of that is behind her, the experience isn't quite forgotten, nor should it be.

"I'm writing a novel now, and it deals with repercussions," she says. "It tells of one woman who is dealing with that sort of discrimination."

"The most challenging thing about being in Ames was how people there and then did not know much about India," she continues. "I had one classmate—who had never been outside of Ames, and while we were in graduate school, she had her first opportunity to leave the country and visit Pakistan as part of a university study group—been in the Peace Corps in Pakistan, and she was and is totally fine. And I have to say, too, that overall I had a wonderful time in Iowa. I made wonderful friends. I had wonderful professors. Everyone I met was very receptive. Until the Gulf War! But even then friendships sustained me."

After Iowa, Visi observed and experienced certain prejudices.

"I met new people 'on the road,'" she says. "Sometimes I'd get a second look and that would unnerve me. I would not know how they would react to me." Not being able to anticipate normal acceptance by another human being can indeed be corrosive. "It got better," Visi is quick to add. "Still, every time there is a global issue . . .!"

What sustains Visi these days, in addition to her upbringing, is her solid marriage, and two children: a daughter, age seven, and a son, who is twelve. Her life as a writer is also deeply fulfilling.

"I work as a freelance writer," she says, "so I'm at home. I'm working on a novel, as I mentioned, as well as a foodie memoir and two children's books. There's a dearth of children's books written by people of colour—I'd like to be part of that change. To tell new and different stories."

Visi's own story, her personal journey, is inspiring. She shows how one's family of origin is key, but that *it is not enough.*

The individual must demonstrate perseverance and show focus in identifying a talent that has to be honed to its top potential.

That being said, I ask Visi, finally, what advise she has to offer Indian students who might want to head to the States for studies. Her response is truly awesome:

"I was one of a handful of women in my grad school group of sixty plus Indian kids who arrived at Iowa State University a couple of decades ago. We had never experienced Pizza Hut pizza or knew what pepperoni was . . . We had only one government run TV channel, so our knowledge of America was based wholly on movies and what we read in books. Today I see so many youngsters from India arriving here to go to undergrad school, and they are filled with confidence and self reliance. Each time I visit India, I am amazed at how much more savvy youngsters are about America and the life here. They have been more exposed to Americanism than we were a couple of decades ago. They already have eaten at a Domino's or a McDonald's or a Subway and can adapt very easily to American pop culture, thanks to T.V., movies, and the media. I'm not sure if that is good or bad, because of the waning 'Indian-ism' among youngsters—they are more American than Indian. Their wallets are fatter now thanks to the earning power of their parents.

"Yet the one thing that they fail to expect is the fact that they have to adapt to a new home and a new way of living. Things function differently here than they do back in India. The general way of life and day-to-day living: lack of domestic help, moral support from family, and a warm parent/sibling to run to during sad moments. Emotional comfort doesn't come easy when one is so far away from home.

"Superficially, things may appear the same, but home is where the heart is. Many who arrive here come with a sense of ambition, yet fail to prepare themselves for that feeling of loneliness that creeps up quite fast. As long as one is prepared for it, one can deal with it."

BEYOND BOLLYWOOD
Pawan Dhingra

Most Americans never make it to India. And while in day-to-day life they may have Indian colleagues, neighbours, and doctors, see Indians on T.V. reporting the news, moderating sports events, talking about medicine, or discussing politics, and perhaps while they may eat in Indian restaurants, what India *is* and what it *means* to be Indian is often a fantasy.

The country and its people are exoticized and stereotypes are attributed to unique individuals with complex histories and lives. Among the most powerful forms of influencing what Americans think about India is Bollywood. Not just the traditional movies geared for Indian audiences, but crossover hits like *Monsoon Wedding* and *Slumdog Millionaire*. While neither film came out of Mumbai studios, both owe a lot to the popular styles of Bollywood movies.

Bollywood's myth-making has its good purposes. Celebration, magic, choreography, style, glamour. As exciting as the Hollywood movies of the 1930s with Fred Astaire and Ginger Rogers, these films create a world that doesn't exist in reality, and make a refuge for all of us who want to get outside ourselves, and a world that can be terrifying. While enjoying a Bollywood movie, we are, for a couple of hours, in a fairy tale without a past or future.

But the reality of the Indian experience cannot be measured by fantasies, and it is left to intellectuals to suss out what is real and what isn't. Through years of fastidious research, a better understanding of what it means to be Indian is now possible.

One of the best-known writers on this phenomenon is Pawan Dhingra, Professor of Sociology and Chair of that department at Tufts University, which is in the Boston area. Born in India, he came to the U.S. as a child, and was raised in Texas.

Still in his late thirties, and looking much younger, Pawan served as a Museum Curator at the Smithsonian Institute in Washington, D.C. from 2011 to 2012, where he co-curated an exhibition, *Beyond Bollywood*. He is also the author of a book on second-generation immigrant communities, *Managing Multicultural Lives: Asian American Professionals and the Challenge of Multiple Identities* (Stanford University Press, 2007). I caught up with Pawan at Amsterdam Falafel, a small franchised restaurant in Davis Square, Somerville where over lunch we talked about his work.

"My first book about immigrant communities looked, in part, at the tensions which exist between professional identity and so-called racial identity," he says. "I looked at college-educated Koreans and Indians, and explored how they constructed identities at home and in civic situations. There's a tension in trying to maintain balance."

As he talks and we enjoy our pita stuffed with falafel and salad, brimming with sauces, the conversation gets lively. Pawan, in addition to his intellect, is a modest, enthusiastic individual capable of speaking with fluency and passion about his ideas. He has had the good fortune to be able to study what goes on around him, and to gather information that will be of great importance to both immigrants as well as those whose communities they have joined.

"We kind of assume immigrant backgrounds," he continues. "But they are more hybrid. And then when an immigrant, say from India, enters the workplace, how does his or her Indian identity show itself? A doctor won't wear traditional Indian clothing at work, but a teacher might. It depends, too, on the authority one has in the workplace. Ultimately, that identity is diluted."

The rich diversity of day-to-day life, both at work and at home, is an exciting realization. It means that identity is not static: people change, adapt, and accentuate certain aspects of their personalities and presentation while keeping other features more circumspect. Overall, Pawan's work implies that there is a great deal of fluidity in how people organize themselves and plan their lives. That, too, can lead to changes with whom immigrants come into contact with: Things indeed go beyond Bollywood, and the *initial* stereotypes North Americans have of Indians give way to realistic observations.

People who meet immigrants change as a result of that contact!

Pawan turns next in our conversation to his year and half as curator at the prestigious Smithsonian Institute. He left academe during that time period in order to create an exhibition that would showcase the variety of India and Indians that had nothing to do with Bollywood.

"We collected a boatload of objects for this," he says. "Like photos of the Indian Spelling Bee winners. And of Indian football players. We brought attention to Dalip Singh Saund— he was the first Indian to serve in the U.S. Congress, and that was long ago, from 1957 to 1962."

He talks of collecting menus of some of the first Indian restaurants in the United States and displaying them in the museum. Of meeting Congressman Saund's grandson. Of the delight he took in the hard work needed to create an exhibition that was the first of its kind in the U.S., and on such a grand scale.

I ask him what he thinks of the bursts of creativity that took place in Indian immigrants who came to the U.S. in the 1970s and after. What are a few of his explanations?

"It's not as exceptional as it sounds," he says. "The 1965 immigration laws brought over highly educated people, and in the continued immigration were many people who were highly skilled in technology. A lot of people who came here, among those highly educated, took advantage of different opportunities. Their talents took them far."

What followed then was that the communities came together and built an impromptu infrastructure. People with comparable aspirations and lifestyles created an environment in which expectations and pressures were shared. The fact that the parents who had come from India were often highly educated meant that they knew what it was like to go to good schools. They knew the value of a first-rate education, and they knew what it takes to get one.

"Day-to-day 'rituals' developed," he says. "The parents set aside time for their kids to study." He smiles between bites of his pita. "And they knew how to enforce rules."

I wonder with him what these pressures did to kids who were not academically inclined or who came from families in the later waves of immigration who were in the mercantile sector. Did they feel left out? Diminished? Is high-level achievement synonymous with what it means to be Indian in America?

"Look at the people who aren't as accomplished," he says. "There remains a connection between taxi drivers and doctors—a lot of Indian doctors came together as Foreign

Medical Graduates, known as FMGs, and formed an inter-ethnic, anti-discrimination organization in the early 1990s." That organization helps those Indians who do not share the same social or economic status as doctors.

So there must have been solidarity based on shared heritage and not just professional success. Being Indian means, in part, looking out for others from India.

"There is an active effort that people put into creating networks and resisting barriers," he says. "It's the same narrative whether the person is a doctor, motel owner, in I.T., or a taxi driver. But it's not a story of ethnicity, per se. This isn't a 'Tiger Mother' story."

Pawan refers to the work of Amy Chua. In her book *Battle Hymn of the Tiger Mother*, Chua, an attorney, put forward the ethnocentric myth that Chinese mothers, by being strict and demanding in their expectations, create children who are hugely successful.

"The real story? The real story," Pawan says, "is the conditions under which people came over. The sector that came over initially and then built support for the next waves of immigrants. And then all of these groups sought to have America live up to its expectations. It's what America is about."

OUR JOURNEY CONTINUES: THE PUBLIC GOOD, MORE MOVIES, THE PHILOSOPHER OF WALL STREET, A MEDIA MOGUL, AND AN ANALYTIC JOURNALIST

FILM-MAKER EXTRAORDINAIRE
Rucha Humnabadkar

"I came to the States in 2001," says film-maker and writer Rucha Humnabadkar, "to attend Carnegie Mellon University, where I got an M.A. in Design. At first I wasn't quite sure what the programme would be about, once on campus I realized it was about 'new media,' which was the early days of user interface design. When I applied, I had studied journalism, written and directed plays in India, and worked in film. The programme at CMU was unique in that it wanted to teach people who were visual to be good with words or people who were good with words to be good with visuals. It took me a semester to get comfortable with the coursework. I had very supportive faculty."

Best known these days for her jury award-winning feature-length movie, *For Here or To Go?*, Rucha arrived at film via a series of unique experiences. The movie captures a generational story, and concerns matters as complex as identity and as practical as visa restrictions. Specifically, as exciting as it may be to want to make use of the cultural and economic freedom of being in the States, there are barriers. If a person is here on a work visa for a company, for example, and wants to stay in the States to start some new enterprise, it can be challenging, to say the least, to remain because the visa is linked to the job. Without the job that allowed them here, they may be subject to deportation.

Rucha's story. Her journey.

"The programme at Carnegie Mellon was what got me here," she says. "But after the first semester I asked myself: 'Is this the right programme for me?" Because it was very different from anything I had done before. I didn't have the luxury of meeting faculty and visiting schools before I arrived to know the details of a programme. In fact, I had never been to the States before!"

Having come from Hyderabad, she found herself in the sprawling, industrial city of Pittsburgh, which is in western Pennsylvania. It's a gritty place, once home of a thriving steel industry, nowadays looking to build an economy that has more components than steel, with pockets of cultural and intellectual depth in its universities, orchestra, and theatre.

Her passion for creative expression seems to have been somewhat stifled by the strictures and demands of a graduate programme. While the programme taught her new skills, left untapped were her interests and resources in creative work. Ironically, it may be that her efforts to reconcile the schooling in the U.S. with what drove her creativity led to imaginative ways of seeing and doing things.

"I wanted to find a way to blend my creative interests and so for my thesis project I analyzed the narrative structure of linear and non-linear films and created a visualization of the same, which met the thesis goal of information architecture and visualization. The head of the design programme was my advisor and thought the idea to be unique and supported me wholeheartedly."

"Every year at our school in India," she says, "we put on a play. Everyone could come. The subjects were often things that everyone knew about." But with original interpretations. "It was great for me. So when I left school in India to come to the States, I really missed that. I used to act, too."

As she describes the life she led before enrolling in a design programme at a prominent U.S. university, Rucha becomes more animated, speaking faster, the words cascading, momentum growing in her voice. Telling stories visually, be it in theatre or film, is clearly what drives her.

"I started my own theatre group," she says. "At the age of about eighteen or nineteen, I was running it at college, in Hyderabad, India."

I wonder where her interest in visual storytelling came from, how she had the confidence at such a young age both to know what it was she wanted to do as well as the discipline needed to do it.

"None of my family has a background in theatre," she explains, "but my family has always been supportive. That's really one of the biggest things in my life. They were of a liberal mindset. I never heard: 'Girls can't do that!' Rather they were very open, and they never stopped me, and, in fact, their support was always there."

Having the strength of family provided Rucha with bulwark needed to stand up to societal norms of prejudice to gender. Whether it was in the States or India, knowing that her family not only believed in her, but implicitly encouraged her to pursue her passion helped her to believe in herself. That belief preceded any evidence of talent, and led in part to her ability to create art with sufficient confidence.

The challenge then became for Rucha: Having identified herself as an artist, having really *become* an artist, how could she integrate that identity with the demands of her programme in the U.S.? The visa restrictions are daunting, to say the least.

If you come to the U.S. as a student, but find that you have other interests, you cannot pursue them full-time (unless you have a green card or become a U.S. citizen). Rucha's own conundrum became the subject of her art.

"When a person from India comes to the U.S. as a student," she says, "an F-1 is issued. It's a student visa. And every time you leave the U.S. to visit India, you hope they let you back in. After graduation, once you find a job you get an H-1B visa, but to maintain status you need to remain with the firm or company that hired you."

When she graduated from Carnegie Mellon, Rucha was hired by eBay, which allowed her to remain in the U.S. But, she notes, there are numerous restrictions.

"Following a so-called 'employment card,'" she says, "there are a number of stages to get your green card. And a lot of people get frustrated. Fortunately for me, eBay had a great legal team and helped every step of the way. Without U.S. citizenship, a person of Indian origin or any immigrant cannot vote, no matter how many years of success or how much money you have."

In the purgatory of immigration, Rucha found herself in a job where the visa restrictions made it hard to give enough time to other interests, but she still held out hope that being in the States would provide her with opportunities to create art. She tempered her frustration with a sense of her own potential. But one can well imagine the difficulty of balancing a dream with the demands of work that distracted her from creative endeavours. "While at my full-time job, which I learned a lot from and which was a wonderful opportunity, I wrote and published my debut novel *Dance of the Fireflies*, based on street kids in India. I would write in the evenings, once I got back from work. Looking back, I found a project I could work on within the confines of the visa system. In fact, having restricted time made me more disciplined.

"I asked myself: 'Do I want to stay or do I want to go back to India?' Opportunities were changing in India." Things were getting better for the work she wanted to do. "It was a dilemma."

Adding to the reality of whether to stay in the U.S. or return to India was an existential dilemma. Not a U.S. citizen, but having developed a new set of ideas by being in the States. Essentially Indian in her cultural framework, but no longer tied to ways she had followed. It is the challenge of the immigrant or near immigrant or kind of stateless person. Indeed, a type of exile.

"I didn't really know where home is," she says. The poignancy of Rucha's observation gives one pause. "I didn't really know where I wanted to be. I asked myself: 'Why am I here in the States?'"

The more Rucha speaks of the situation in which she found herself, the better the sense one gets from listening to her that it takes enormous personal courage to withstand both the practical considerations of the visa problem as well as the existential dilemma that results. Those individuals who are capable of reconciling all of the challenges stand a chance of success in the U.S. But that requires stamina, patience, confidence, and an ability to delay gratification. The immediate situation of the immigrant in purgatory can be debilitating.

"The visa situation stifles growth," Rucha says simply, "and a lot of people are stuck for a long time." She describes further the uniqueness of her own time. "When one is hired as an individual contributor, one cannot switch companies or roles easily on an H1-B visa. The goal is to get a green card if you want to have a life here. You absolutely have to make that happen. Or . . . or you're going back."

RACE, SEXUALITY, IDENTITY

Arun Venugopal

How do values get transmitted from one generation to the next? So many Indians who were born in this country assimilated, and became Americans in every sense, but at the same time were able to retain the values of a mother country with which they had limited direct experience. Certainly their families—through language, holidays, food, style of dress, literature, and art—were able to introduce Indian values to their children. But tangibly, as they entered U.S. society, and became as American as they were Indian, how did the values of another culture stay alive? And how, in practical, day-to-day behaviours, are those values expressed?

Values from one immigrant home to the next vary, of course, and the question is really one of specificity. If the original Indian household was, for example, one in which parents were religious, the children may feel some obligation to maintain that affiliation as adults. More complex are subtle values having to do with justice, empathy, and a demotic outlook.

Arun Venugopal is a passionate, engaged thinker, now living in Queens, New York City, who grew up in Houston, Texas, and along the way to where he is now, he returned with his family to India. His story is one of biculturalism, which is increasingly the case in this age of relatively affordable travel between India and the U.S. What happens to identity from this cross-fertilization is rarely a muddle. Rather, it is a rich mosaic of ideas and behaviours from two cultures.

"I grew up in Texas," Arun says. He speaks so quickly that I have a hard time keeping up with him. "My father is now retired, but he was an allergist and immunologist, an asthma specialist, who was offered a job. But in 1983, when I was ten, we moved back to Chennai. The plan at that point was to stay—not to move back to the U.S. We had returned to India for a variety of reasons, including professional opportunities and to maintain a connection to family—my father is one of seven kids and so is my mother. We moved only a few hundred miles from Kerala, which is where the family originated. And my father was given the opportunity to start a world-class hospital. But after three years we moved back, because he could not sell the house in Houston."

Having a family from Kerala, where a degree of political vibrancy and change were apparent for over half a century since Independence, had an impact on Arun despite not having grown up there. He speaks of his grandparents and the extended families of both his mother and father in that state. Then he turns somewhat abruptly to his own work, but the shift makes sense: there is a strong connection between what he believes in and where he came from.

"I'm a journalist," he shares, "and my work concerns issues of race, identity, oppression, and marginalization among other things. I'm also interested in considering multiple political viewpoints, and issues of immigration. Within the context of the Indian American community in the U.S., I wonder: What is a successful minority? What does that mean? What are the challenges of acculturation?"

Arun's passion is his own, but as we talk further, it becomes apparent that it's having a family background from a state in India known for its political outspokenness that influenced him. Specific family members had a big role in shaping him, too.

"My uncle, who passed away a few years ago, was a journalist in Kerala," he says. "And my wife's father was a journalist. Me? I feel as if I stumbled into journalism. I was always interested in culture. And at Trinity University in San Antonio, Texas, where I got my degree, I studied religion as well as communications, which was my major. For me, religion was a very interesting way of getting at culture. I took an intellectual perspective regarding it."

From a more practical point of view, however, finding work with degrees in religion and communication can be very challenging. Especially for an abstract thinker whose passion for knowledge was in the foreground. So what does an Indian American intellectual do in the heart of Texas?

"I moved to India," says Arun. College had ended. "I was there for close to four years, and I worked then as a copywriter in Bangalore. I also worked on the set of a film—there's a loose family connection we have to Deepa Mehta—about the partition of India, called *Earth*. Deepa was the director." He laughs. "I was made the assistant to the assistant director. And it was a great job! Aamir Khan starred in the movie; he's one of India's biggest actors."

But while Arun was in India, trying to figure out what to do with his life, his parents were in the States. It was an ironic reversal of the immigration experience.

"My parents were like, 'Are you ever going to move back?' But I had no aim or direction." He seems to have been happy in India not knowing what to do next, and not having any financial obligations like a mortgage, or a wife or children. "I found work at one of the best ad agencies in India. It was all very good. This was the mid-nineties and there were thirty to forty per cent pay raises happening. I was young and without any real cares. So naturally my parents got worried."

What did his parents do with their wayward son who had returned to the mother country? He, who was eschewing The American Dream. What could they do to help him when it was clear that not only didn't he want the help, he didn't really need it.

"My parents deployed some uncle-type figure," he recalls mirthfully. "And he talked to me, saying 'Your parents are really worried about you,' etc."

Eventually, Arun returned to the States. What did he learn from his years in India? What did he take with him that helped him succeed as an American?

"The time in India helped me," he says. "It got me out of my comfort zone for one thing. For instance, I stopped taking ideas for granted. I had grown up in a privileged household, and in India I worked in settings with people who did not have what I had. And I had conversations with Indians about the States. I remember one person from the office who blindsided me with a question: 'Are all blacks thieves in America?' The images broadcast around the world created that impression. I was so startled by his question that I've never forgotten it." All this fit in with Arun's love of and intrigue with communication. "I thought more about media. How news sites reflect a certain kind of viewpoint. It can be a homogenized view. It can exert cultural power like *BuzzFeed, Jezebel,* and *Huffington Post.* There can be a way of framing things from the headlines down, and I saw it mimicked in the Indian news media in a kind of slavish way. There was, overall, a loss of diversity."

The loss of diverse viewpoints in media sparked Arun's way of seeing things, and gradually he must have realized how it could be possible for someone like himself, at home literally in two cultures, to provide what was missing. By being part of India *and* America, he saw things others who were mono-cultural did not.

Arun returned to the United States in the spring of 1998. How had he changed?

"It was a slow evolution," he says. "I had never thought of myself as a journalist. It took years after college for that to happen." And being independent in India. "Advertising was a stop along the way; it was fun while it lasted. And these last few years, things have coalesced."

Arun has a lively sense of humour, perhaps enhanced due to his being so much of an observer, and he balances this with a focus in his writing on very serious matters. It's what helps make his reporting, featured regularly on *WNYC*, New York public radio, and on nationally syndicated public radio shows like *All Things Considered* and *Morning Edition* as well as in *The Guardian* and *The Wall Street Journal*, so valuable and unique. He examines the human dimension in deep economic and societal problems. Such as racism.

"Being brown and having lived in India has influenced my thinking," he says. "It's a constant conversation. And it's possible, if you're brown, and an Indian American, to use being different from the mainstream as a position from which to reflect on things. You gain a certain credibility. Because you have a position of difference."

Again, Arun contemplates life with many lenses. Not just through colour, culture, or family. But through roots that go back to his family's origins. In Kerala. Maybe there's a certain cynicism from this state, a slight suspicion of the established order that can fuel journalism.

"Kerala was democratic," Arun points out, "when a communist government was voted in, which led to land reform. Vast swaths of state land owned by the Nair caste came undone when the communists took over. That's only a couple of generations removed. My grandmother was in that caste and she'd say things like, 'We used to own *all that* over there.' That made me conscious of my place in a larger power structure. It's not abstract. I felt, first-hand, the fundamental process of wealth and power in the world."

And then, too, removed from the political process was the intimacy of Arun's own home.

"I constantly think: Why was my dad successful? It helps to have been given a highly subsidized education. And my parents really had to struggle—like I said, they were each one of seven siblings. There was pressure to provide for younger siblings as well."

Arun goes back and forth between the political and the personal as he speaks, and the forcefulness of his thinking comes from this weaving together. It was Kerala that shaped him even from a generational distance; it was his parents whose perseverance was inspiring. And nowadays, living in New York City, fully engaged with today's world rather than nostalgic about the past or cloistered within his own ethnicity, Arun takes the panoply of experiences and analyzes current events through his reporting.

He notes how the 1965 immigration laws enabled Indians to come to this country with fewer conditions.

"LBJ really changed things," he says. "It wouldn't have happened earlier. Think about the Asian Exclusion Act!" He refers to the race-based legislation of 1924 that kept Asians out of the U.S. "My father benefitted from the 1965 laws. He came with a medical degree."

The racism of federal policies, and in communities, created psychological conditions that might be described as empathic. Having experienced the effects of a racist culture, numerous diverse groups could find common ground. Each group, though separate and unique, had in common the experience of having been discriminated against by the so-called white majority. That commonality can lead to empathy for one another that, in turn, is a building block for coalitions.

"Non-black activists of colour after Ferguson tried to forge alliances," Arun says. "Arab-Americans. South Asians. It's important to understand the experiences of African-Americans. A form of solidarity."

The success of his own community might also be somewhat of a template for others.

"There are reasons for the success," Arun says. "There's pride in a competitive spirit, for example. Like all the Indian American kids who win spelling bees! Something does happen within the community that reinforces a virtuous cycle of competition and achievement. But then the question is: How do we perpetuate high *ideals*? What are the dynamics in this narrative?"

Although Arun lives in Jackson Heights, Queens, which he describes as originally having been 'an Indian American enclave,' he is part of New York City. This means reporting on the tumult and frisson of one of the world's most diverse cities. That's the scene, that's what's happening. And because of his own cultural diversity, Arun is uniquely suited to observe what goes on around him.

That is a fundamental part of the culture that was transmitted to him from his father, mother, and grandparents—an openness to life and a willingness and desire for change.

"Why is this possible?" Arun asks rhetorically with a smile. "A gay pride parade and down the street at the same time women in burkhas? It's all fun. It's fascinating!"

He adds, in a more serious, contemplative tone: "The United States, and the Western world in general, are undergoing a traumatic process at the moment. As we're witnessing all around us, there is a lot of resistance to the notion of diversity that so many of us have held up for years, idealized in fact. Where is this resistance coming from, and how is it going to play out? Those of us who have grown up in immigrant cultures, hybrid cultures, clearly have a vested interest in the outcome. But we're also especially well-equipped to understand what's happening, and help shape society for the better."

MEDIA MOGUL
Ninan Chacko

As CEO of PR Newswire, a global communications and marketing provider, Ninan Chacko, runs a business that establishes and nurtures ties on all of the world's continents, erasing borders, bringing people together, identifying and establishing affiliations which transcend race, religion, gender, class, caste, and nation. With a newswire database of 10,700 syndicated websites and 543,379 journalists in its world-wide network, PR Newswire is in a formidable, billion dollar industry (PR Newswire's own revenue is about a third of a billion but it sits in a multi-billion dollar industry.) with deep and not always obvious influence on information used in making news and sharing knowledge. Who is Ninan Chacko?

"The definition of my identity is a very interesting question," Ninan says jovially. "I'm ethnically from Kerala, but my father was born and brought up in Malaysia, as was I. So I was in Malaysia as well through second grade, then studied in India for five years, and wound up in the U.K. at a boarding school." He lives internationally these days as well, and the influences on him are not just professional. "My wife is from Colombia. Italian-Spanish. So there's the classic question people ask me: 'Where are you from?' I always say: New York."

Indeed, Ninan's ability to help build and run a global enterprise, one which obviates constrictive and almost outdated notions of identity that were formed tribally, is heartfelt. His fascination for common ground, and his ability to achieve isn't abstract: Malaysia, India, England, New York City. All of these places make up who he is and evolving as a person, and that transformation shows up in his work, interests, and outlook on life. And further, his enthusiasm and life serve as inspiration for others seeking to transcend the definitions placed upon them by those wedded to the past.

"I self-identify as an American," Ninan continues, "and I happen to be of Malaysian birth and Indian origin."

His amalgam of identities derives from real and very personal experiences. Not only did he grow up through adolescence in three different countries, he came to the United States at an early age. One can't help but think that Ninan is ideally suited to live in this age of globalization. His background, too, as an Indian, coming from a multi-ethnic society, provided him with the confidence and familiarity that were needed to adapt to new cultures wherever he found them.

He did not resist change. On the contrary, he embraced it. As an Indian who was educated in India, living in Bangalore for five years, and then Malaysia, he was accustomed to being part fo the day-to-day of a community. In the U.K., he found himself part of a minority, but a significant one. Then he came to the States.

"I was about seventeen years old when I came here for college in 1982," he says. "To the University of Kansas in the Midwest. I was straight out of boarding school in the U.K." The shift from one culture to the next could not have been easy, and while Ninan gained strength from each experience, what was it like in terms of his development of identity? He was at a vulnerable age when he arrived in the States, at a time developmentally when teenagers try to figure out just who they are: Who am I? "The most essential notion of identity for me is the idea of America. I love the freedom that can come from that."

The cultural flexibility of America fit in nicely with Ninan's personal challenges. He also had the good fortune not only to come from a country that is multi-ethnic, but to have a family with the socio-economic status which is a natural foundation for personal confidence.

"Both my parents are doctors," Ninan explains. They lived well abroad. "We were in Penang in Malaysia. It was beautiful there. The beaches. And practically the best food in the world!" He laughed as he reminisced about delicious meals. "I was the youngest of four. And at around age eight, we were sent to live with our grandparents in Bangalore for five years. This was the early '70s, and what prompted that decision were changes in Malaysia. The government changed the English language instruction in schools to Malay. My parents didn't find that particularly helpful."

At the time Ninan arrived in Bangalore, the city and region were hardly developed. He was at home, but he was not at home.

"It was a sleepy backwater then," he says. "Sort of the Florida of India. No T.V. And I was a foreign student with a Malaysian passport!"

At the same as he experienced a change, it wasn't quite an alienation. He was Indian. He had family. He looked like most of the people around him.

More powerful changes took place when Ninan left Asia.

"At boarding school in the U.K. there was racism and there were stereotypes. I had experienced some racism," he says reluctantly. But his positive outlook on life steeled him as did certain pragmatic features. "Education had prepared me. English was my mother tongue. And then when I came to the U.S., Lawrence, Kansas, where the university is located, it turned out to be a liberal enclave—where you are who you are depends on what you can do." The experience of relative meritocracy must have been thrilling, bracing, and inspiring. It wasn't what he was used to. "No stereotype was applied to me."

"My family is part of the Syrian Christian Church of St. Thomas," Ninan says. And then there are other potentially divisive aspects to his identity before coming to the U.S. "Skin colour, caste—less applicable to me, more so religion, family background. But I can't think that way. I also can't think of other countries that are like this one."

Where what you do defines you as a person rather than a perception of where you came from or some ill-defined notion of what your potential is based on your so-called race, caste, class, gender, religion, or ethnicity.

"The U.S. is the only place in my experience where the stereotypes don't come into play," he says. "There is a lack of tribalism here. Further, the pace and rate of evolution of this in the U.S. has been heartening. You also see it globally." As ideas spread. "London, of course, has become multi-cultural."

How all of these powerful influences and experiences shaped Ninan's personality become clear as he speaks about his remarkable journey across three continents. He took the personal to the professional.

"As CEO of PR Newswire, I manage a distribution network," he says modestly. "Originally, we were sort of a grassroots organization compiling press releases of companies and delving into communication. It was the old days of pure advertising. Nowadays, it's a rich, nuanced story. We have tens of thousands of websites co-mingled with editorial content. Using social media."

Was he always a media mogul?

"No, I was trained as an aerospace engineer," explains Ninan. "The bulk of my career was in the travel and transportation industry. I have a tech background, and my degree is in aircraft design. My graduate research was sponsored by NASA &

GE." After eight months in the airline operations engineering arena, Ninan moved to management, focusing there on IT and travel distribution. "I stayed for twenty years, and worked on commercial areas, outsourcing, private equity, and so on."

Ninan is particularly adept at discovering links between people and systems that can be joined through management. His genius resides in being able to think with flexibility and to organize systems, and there is little doubt that his own global experiences helped to shape his versatile and open-minded way of doing things.

Yet, being Indian made him who he is today; and, he sees ongoing changes there which suggest a reciprocal relationship between those who, like him, left and those who remained. These changes come from influences from around the world via Indians living abroad who communicate with family there. Then, as India changes, those living abroad change, too. It's an exciting, organic process, and a time of enormous change within India and around the world.

"Things are changing in India," he says. "Greater creativity, work ethic, and," he laughs, "luck!"

The combination of the personal and professional pushes Ninan along. He seeks new challenges as he progresses.

"I'm learning to lead," he says. "To motivate. To move teams. I'm not really a start-up person; I'm more fascinated, and always have been, by international business."

Where is Ninan's future? Wherever his extraordinary skills and interests take him, he is explicit about the pivotal role being educated, working, and living in the United States has had on his personal and professional development. He identifies certain national characteristics which he has taken to heart, for example.

"I'm enormously optimistic about America," he says. "There is a true exceptionalism here. Economic freedom within borders. A place that is a magnet for talent, and the most powerful engine anywhere on the globe."

He's not chauvinistic about the U.S. Rather, Ninan thinks of the country as having identifiable assets that can be utilized by those with drive, talent, focus, and luck.

"There is cultural fluency and fluidity here," he says, "which can be felt even greater if one comes here as an undergraduate, as I did." Coming as graduate students or employees, immigrants may miss out on the socialization and acculturation that take place when still adolescents. "They don't have the same verve and ease. Whereas undergrads are interwoven into the fabric of the U.S. And remember: when I first got started here, Indians were not CEOs or senior management." Maybe growing into an adult with fellow Americans gave Ninan an important sense of fitting in. "Today you have the opposite stereotype."

Ninan really benefitted from the rare experience of being part of three very broadly defined cultures—Indian, British, and American—and while being able to cherry-pick from each what he felt to be the best, he didn't really belong wholeheartedly to either. An insider, an outsider, a global citizen, a New Yorker, Ninan is truly a 21st century person.

"I was the beneficiary of the British educational system with roots in the Victorian era," he said. "The English are awfully good at separating the truly bright from everyone else.

In my English school, a lot of emphasis was placed on the art of inquiry and writing." Ninan is not being hubristic; he's just describing what it was like to be identified at a young age as a person with talent. Just being identified is never enough. The rest was up to him. And that's where the States came in. "Then the U.S. educational system provided me with a work ethic," he says. "So I felt in the U.K. having been lifted up and separated due to what teachers felt were really good skills. It was through a funny mix of a colonial educational system and the U.S. system . . ." He pauses. "It was like the wheat from the chaff and then a work ethic was added!"

Both educational systems, to varying degrees, had some core belief in merit. However, Ninan implies that the English system while identifying talent did not turn as blind an eye to matters of a person's perceived background quite as much as the U.S. did. In the States, talent can be unleashed. There are, in his opinion and experience, fewer stereotypes applied to Indians than in England.

"I've always been fascinated by people who have succeeded through the American experience," he says. He notes the altruism that at its best the U.S. has made a part of becoming an American. That seems to be connected to a view of society less insular and less tribal than others. The caring applies to human beings, and not just those with whom Americans feel affiliation based on race, class, or gender. "The idea of charitable giving. Or empathy. On a bigger scale, the Voice of America and the Marshall Plan."

His love of the States is informed by his success here, but Ninan is also able to appreciate how potential in individuals in the U.S. can be understood and pushed along. He feels as if this is the best place at this moment in history for that to happen, but his point isn't to trumpet one nation over another. He seems to think instead that the U.S. might inspire other nations to inculcate the power of merit over tribal concerns.

"There's an uncertain mix of things in the environment in America," Ninan concludes. "But overall it's here that the cream is skimmed. It's a place where you will see rewards reaped twenty years from now in everything."

THE PHILOSOPHER OF WALL STREET AND THE ART OF THE DEAL
Billy Rao

So many brainy people live abstract, dreamy lives, contemplative and on the sidelines, analytical about the action on the field, but not Billy Rao. Using his high-powered intellect in the world of business, he is a roaring success as he combines strands of seemingly disparate knowledge and experience to create an utterly unique life in finance where millions and millions *and millions* of dollars are as routine for him as grains of rice are to a farmer. But where he stands out from most others in the business world is his commitment to ideals rooted in the very unusual education he had in India.

"I'm from Hyderabad," he says. Now he lives in New York City. "And although I later attended the Indian Institute of Technology in Madras for engineering, and then the Ivy League institution of Columbia University and then the Stern Business School at NYU, it was my boarding school that really shaped me the most."

Billy modestly glosses over the education he had after boarding school, but with a little prodding he admits to being (ABD—all but dissertation) in Business from NYU in New York City. And, yes, he made a small fortune on Wall Street starting with Bear Stearns and others as an expert in arbitrage, quantitative analysis, high frequency trading, and hedge funds.

"But I want to talk to you about my boarding school," Billy says, and it's clear from his fervour that he is speaking from the heart. "It was a Krishnamurthy School." He refers to the famous educational project established by the great Indian philosopher J. Krishnamurthy. So much of the philosophy imbued in teaching there, organization of the classroom, appreciation for both the individual and community—all these matters, especially for a young child, can have a lasting impact on his or her forming of personality. And with Billy, the impact, the love he felt, is something he has kept alive throughout his time doing business. It can be an unsettling contradiction, this contrast between cut-throat business dealings and the art of learning. Or it can be the framework for a powerful and worthy struggle to be original. "Understanding was the thing at school. Empowering the individual. A love of learning. It was all very beneficial to me."

At Nehru Zoological Park, Hyderabad: Wishing to pet the tiger in a zoo sans fences.

Watching a Krishnamurthy lecture at home with a friend,
on Central Park South, New York City.

I'm trying to understand the links between the philosophy he was taught as a child and the things he needed to learn to do business on Wall Street. Though it isn't at all clear yet, Billy knows how it all fits together, so it's best to let him tell his story the way he wants to tell it. He's a man used to shaping his own narrative rather than allowing others to tell him who he is or isn't.

"It was around 1985 or 1986," he continues, "and quantitative techniques were just getting used on Wall Street. Very structured data, which allowed for faster processing of trades, especially in the derivatives and futures markets. And personally, what influenced me, was a certain kind of balance, which I attribute to being exposed to the philosophy of Krishnamurthy." I'm beginning to see his point. What he means is that Krishnamurthy's philosophy, in part, held that observation must precede action or reaction. The individual can choose to respond based on knowledge, but should wait until the information coming in provides what's needed to make a thoughtful, informed response. Abstractly, this means a contemplative life with decision making that is at times unhurried. But applied to deal-making in business, it allows for a well-conceived, pinpoint precision in closing deals. It's an intellectual approach rather than one that is emotional. "Krishnamurthy's teachings brought exposure to how the human mind works. How you can react. Is it from jealousy? Competitiveness? What is the path to truth? It was about learning about yourself."

His time at a Krishnamurthy School isn't soaked with nostalgia for Billy, nor is it recalled as an idyll. It was time of growth when ideas seeped into him in a setting where learning was pleasurable. Unlike so many schools where discipline and rote lessons are the norm, where students are kept silent unless called upon, here was an environment designed to help people identity what made them most human and feel most alive.

"It was a heterogeneous school," Billy says, "with kids from the Middle East, the United States, Australia, Canada, and so on. Yes, there was an underlying common background in that students came from a better economic strata. That was a plus in a sense: to start off things in a certain way." The school was a world apart. "We had no access to the outside world. And within the school, in addition to what we were taught, we had a phenomenal music programme. International music. We had the best musicians performing. And teaching." Not just music: the arts. The emphasis was on being creative with one's knowledge of self and the world. Not to take facts and insight and leave them on the page, but to give these expression. "The drama programme was amazing. Our drama teacher was Roshan Seth, who became the famous actor who played Nehru in the Gandhi movie. And, overall, because of their associations with Krishnamurthy, the lectures and interactions had underlying philosophy. We all became very well acquainted with international figures. On top of everything, Krishnamurthy would come to the school for three or three and a half months each year, and we saw and listened to him almost twice a week."

It wasn't just the teachers or the fame of those illustrious ones who came to visit and spend time with the kids. There was an overriding sense of being different from the rest of India and the world. Feeling that their education made them different, the kids took pride in themselves and the school. A rather different experience than most kids whose schools tend to be factory-like and strictly hierarchical. It may be that this open-minded approach to learning turned out students who saw things differently, too.

"There were no uniforms," Billy recalls. "Little need for discipline. No rankings. No religion. Absolutely no religious bent: no mosque, no temple, no church. In part, the idea was to take the responsibility for educating yourself. There's a book about Krishnamurthy that explains so much about his outlook. It is titled *Krishnamurthy: The Years of Awakening*. His idea was that the path to the truth cannot be achieved institutionally. He decided to go around the world and empower the individual. The point was: individualism, not institutions."

When Krishnamurthy visited the school, Billy had the first-hand opportunity to experience time with one of the twentieth century's most important philosophers. The impact on a young boy is incalculable.

"He would take walks at 4 p.m.," Billy recalls fondly, "and take two or three students with him." I'm picturing this great man with kids in tow listening to his every word, rapt and in awe. "He was not a big believer in competition. He believed you could accomplish whatever you want if you understand really well. One of the things that appealed to me was this: if you really do well, it becomes an aesthetic."

Indeed, the art of the deal.

"When you're doing your best," Billy continues, "it really is an aesthetic! Those teachings were very useful to me. The beauty and aesthetics of doing well: That's what makes you happy in the real world. Not metrics. As a human being, I don't measure success or lack of success. There are no parameters. I want instead an individual aesthetic and to do that," and this is key, "you have to interact with a community."

So the individualism, creativity, and freedom inculcated in Billy as a child took root, and then found fruition in a broader context. This isn't a philosophy meant to justify selfishness; it is a way of being that contextualizes achievement in each individual through their own success as seen in their ability to make connections in the world. It's complex sounding, but in reality it is quite practical when applied to Wall Street.

"Questions arise," Billy says. "Such as: 'How do you handle your anger? How do you handle your emotions?' The real acceptance has to come within yourself." Through self-control, Billy implies, one has greater strength and reserve needed for observation which must precede decision making. "It boils down to communication within oneself and within the environment. And in today's world, people who can communicate multi-culturally can achieve more for themselves and others. You have to train yourself."

The more Billy elucidates his views, the more clear it is that although he is a successful business person in every sense, his upbringing in an Indian school established by a philosopher deeply informed not just his thinking, but his entire personality. He is a rare and sincere person of depth: a thinking banker.

"I have positive views of the world," he says. "That part of me makes it very easy to interact with others. The positive views are part of my self evolution, and one aspect of that is when I experience a setback or failure, I don't blame it on others. Further, I've moved away from what was a corporate path to one that is characterized by entrepreneurial effort. I worked for big corporations, and advised and set them up in India, but now I'm going in a different direction." He pauses. "My real passion is to create an aesthetic environment for education. The whole process. To change schools where they hear, but don't listen."

Billy is taking what he learned, embraced, and loved as a child in India and, having applied it to the business world, is now being more personal about where things stand in his life, and what he wants to accomplish next.

"My views have evolved over the past fifteen years," he says. "I ask myself, 'What do we need to know?' I think we need to develop a skill and higher analytical abilities. These are needed to sieve through information." Indeed, there is a glut of facts and opinions on the Internet with no weight attached to any datum, per se, such that the world can seem to be an amorphous place. Where Kim Kardashian is front-page news next to an article about ISIS. "I'm pursuing a project. I want to set up educational environments. Special centres that can provide technical knowledge: how to learn. How to assimilate and build aesthetics. The focus would be on processing skills, not storage skills."

So much of education is having students memorize material and repeat it back to a teacher. There is little questioning of what is to be memorized, scant interaction between students, and almost no conceptual thinking. Because Billy had the privilege and luck to attend a school at an early, impressionable age where he was taught to think and be creative, he can imagine another way.

With all this contemplation of his own education and the future, I wonder what advice Billy has for young Indians planning on coming to the U.S. to pursue *their* ambitions. And what qualities might these individuals need, what might they contribute to their cultures here and at home?

"Indians have great training culturally," Billy says enthusiastically. "Educationally, the standards are very high. But at the same time, many spend their time with a limited view of what's really going on. Is it lack of knowledge? Is it the culture? Those who come to the U.S. for higher education have the opportunity to evolve in terms of their personalities by interacting with Americans. So I'd say assimilate, don't build a cocoon or shell. Drop the close-minded approach. Don't be inhibited to the possibilities of experiences."

Billy routinely takes the personal and sees dimensions of his own life that, insightfully, might apply to others. He offers advice that he has given himself.

"I dropped a lot of things that influenced me in India," he says. He laughs. "Sloppiness, for one thing. One of the keys in order to succeed is that you also have to assimilate things here. You have to be very open. There is exposure to a different society than the one you're used to. Frankly, in India you're built around a base called fear. As in: 'Don't do this! Don't do that!'" He smiled with excitement at the life he has made for himself, and which continues to evolve as he works on the task of integrating philosophy with pragmatism. He is fortunate to have a sense of purpose. "But here, in the States, you have to take risks. That's what American culture teaches."

Open to learning no matter where he is due to the foundation he was given at school in India. Krishnamurthy would be proud of his pupil.

FOLLOW THE MONEY
Gita Gopinath

Harvard University's Department of Economics is housed inside the stern looking Littauer Center, just off of Harvard Yard, beside Harvard Law School, within Harvard Square, and beside the Cambridge Common. It's here that current and past policies are scrutinized and taught, and where tomorrow's world leaders emerge to take positions at the most important institutions on the planet. Money, which is as complex, scary, depressing, and life-changing as sex, is here approached with fearlessness and deep curiosity. Economists have a reputation for being disconnected from the arts, but no group is more creative, versatile in thinking, and brave in their willingness to confront the bugaboo of money. Money is the thing that we are taught not to talk about—along with religion and sex—but economists recognize that no other subject has more bearing on our personalities and societies. As Cyndi Lauper put it in her pop song of long ago, money changes everything.

Gita Gopinath is one of the stars of the department at Harvard, and in her small, austere office, great ideas are being generated that have the potential to change our lives. Down to earth, capable of explaining complicated ideas in ways which simplify them, Gita is among those who combine a willingness to recognize the human factor in economics with analysis of the market forces that shape all of us.

"If someone in India asks me where I am from, I say Kerala, because my parents are from Kerala," she says, "but actually I grew up in Mysore." Gita thinks of it as a small town, in some respects. "My father is a small-scale industrialist there—he loves challenges and loves starting new things, he's always finding new passions. And he loves India. He's from the generation born before Independence so he's intensely patriotic."

The family's move from Kerala is far from unusual. Many go to the Gulf for work opportunities as well.

From Mysore, Gita went to Delhi. It was there that she achieved a B.A. in economics from Delhi University and subsequently an M.A. in the same field. Then it was time to get her Ph.D.

"I started out at the University of Washington in Seattle," Gita says happily, as she recalls the halcyon days of being a young student in a country she had never visited before. "It was great! The city is so beautiful—I felt as if I was in a Bollywood movie! And the university had organized a host family for me, which helped. It was a woman originally from Pakistan. She picked me up from the airport. I'm terribly disorganized, I've always been absent-minded, and she was a support." The absent-minded professor! As if. Gita is one of the youngest tenured professors in the history of Harvard. "The host family was perfect for making the transition."

But why leave India for the U.S. in the first place?

"Remember it was the early 1990s," she says, "and India was just starting its reforms. Further, there were not a lot of job opportunities." She wasn't the only one to leave home. "About a third of my class in Delhi left for the U.S. There was no job market in India."

Indeed, Gita's appreciation for the ways in which economics affects our lives is visceral rather than abstract. She has a pragmatic view of things based on personal experience: her father left Kerala for work. She left Delhi for education and work.

"Being in Seattle was wonderful," she recalls. "I used to get immense grief in India for being absent-minded. I'd get yelled at for not being prepared or being forgetful. Not in Seattle. It was more relaxed." She laughs. "Maybe a West Coast vibe. But I don't mean," she is quick to add, "that it's better or worse, it's just cultural. And another thing that's cultural, too—people here are thinking about themselves mostly. So how I behaved wasn't as important to them."

Seattle was also oddly familiar.

"In many cases, foreign students were the majority in our classes," Gita says. "Many people were students who didn't grow up in the U.S."

But after a year at the University of Washington, Gita had the opportunity to continue her studies at Princeton University.

After five years there, under the tutelage of some of the world's most famous economists, including Ben Bernanke (former chairman of the Federal Reserve) and Kenneth Rogoff (a former director of research at the International Monetary Fund [IMF]), she achieved her doctorate.

After Princeton, Gita taught at the University of Chicago, in its business school, and in 2005 she arrived at Harvard.

Currently, Gita is working on a few monumental projects, and it's good to listen closely since her research has the potential to create reverberations in many people's daily lives.

"I'm studying government debt," Gita shares. "Government debt, for example, as it relates to monetary unions as in the EU. There are different levels of government debt, and I'm interested in what kind of frictions monetary policy can cause in that context. The original framing of EU monetary policy was that you couldn't buy back debt—there would be no lending in a crisis. That of course turned out to be a big problem. So I am researching this question: Under what circumstances should monetary intervention take place? When you have a self-fulfilling crisis, markets think you'll be in a mess, and then it's harder to borrow." Plus, because of EU regulations against lending! "But that's when intervention should take place in order to reduce debt. To reduce the panic of investors." So in order to reduce debt within EU guidelines, economic policy has to be innovative. "Fiscal devaluations are permitted," Gita says. "These would mimic currency devaluations, which are not permitted, by decreasing payroll taxes and increasing value-added tax."

Gita is also focused, for the past ten years, on the links between prices and exchange rates, capital flows, and misallocation of funds as it pertains to loss of productivity.

From her description of economics, the fascination she has is contagious. She makes the subject come alive in ways that make it apparent that money can not only be understood, but that not doing so, as the economist Thomas Piketty has noted, is at one's own peril. (His book, *Capital,* is on her bookshelf beside me.) Decisions about the way we live are being made by powerful individuals without regard for the effect of policies—look at the turmoil in Greece or China—and Gita's work is fundamental in making what is obscure more transparent. Does she come from a background of economics?

"It was complete chance that I became an economist," Gita says. "I studied science through twelfth grade, and growing up in Mysore that path usually means that a person will go into engineering, medicine, or the administrative service. I wasn't wedded to engineering or medicine. My father was taken with the idea of elite government service, and studying economics at Delhi University was felt to be an advantage in that regard. The idea was that I was going to study there and then three to five years later take the exam for the Indian civil services. But I just enjoyed economics a lot. I've always enjoyed science and math as well, and economics uses a lot of tools from math."

Then what happened was that India experienced an economic crisis around the same time—this was between 1989 and 1992. What Gita was studying in the classroom had real meaning on the streets and in people's homes.

"The crisis was simply about the fact that there was not enough money coming in to finance our imports," Gita says. "There was a loss of confidence, monetarily, in India. So the IMF came in with money and conditions."

This unusual juncture of academic study and economic turmoil in the world around her must have helped to shape her decision to hunker down and pursue what has become an illustrious career in economics.

"I just like the idea of getting very deep into a topic," Gita says rather modestly.

Added to living through a period of economic synergy was Gita's family background, which provided her with intimate and historical reasons for her success.

"My father is super-duper," Gita says proudly. "He and my mother had just the two daughters, and he gave me all the ambition I needed: 'Work hard and get what you want.'" Gita also looks to her social position. "I come from matriarchal societies. On my mother's side, we are Nair. On my father's side, we are Nambiar. The family name and property in the caste are in the mother's name. It's not completely equal between males and females in these groupings, but being a girl was what people wanted. I never got a sense that as a girl I was second-class. I even had uncles and aunts who had multiple kids because they kept wanting to have a daughter." She pauses thoughtfully. "Therefore, I had a different mindset than other kids. I was made to feel that I was incredibly valuable to society. And having that combination of a belief in hard work and then coming to the U.S. where it will actually be possible was a great opportunity!"

Given the uniqueness of her background, upbringing, and sheer intellect, I wonder what advice Gita might offer in a general sense to those coming these days to America.

"Eighteen- to twenty-year-old's know so much about America already," she says. "They have so much information. That's a huge plus. To add to that, I'd say that the most important thing is respect. That everyone must treat you with respect here. Don't expect or allow less. When I moved from Mysore to Delhi, the culture was very different. But I was never apologetic about being from a small town. And here I'm never apologetic about coming from India. There's an unfortunate tendency to second-guess yourself coming from another country, but don't do it. I would also say this to new immigrants: never feel lesser about yourself."

FROM INDIA WITH LOVE AND BACK AGAIN
Shveta Raina

Many of the success stories people tell about their lives involve a difficult struggle to create a new life in America. To move to another country, add the values of that place to an existing repertoire, assimilate, and look back on what was a prior foundation that has been built upon. The deep love and respect for heritage is balanced by a thankful look forward: Building a life in America, no matter how talented or hard working the immigrant, is fraught with unpredictability, cultural misunderstandings in both directions, and a sense of abandonment. It's exciting to become an American, but in that transformation the past can be muddied or even lost.

But these days, for a younger generation of Indians, it need not be, and it isn't for many, one identity or another. Some people don't have to choose. The versatility and fluidity of cultures, nations, information, and knowledge are evident. The Internet and Skype allow an individual to be virtually in two places at one time. And for those immigrants who have the skills and desire to work physically in both places, India and the States, affordable airfares and infrastructures exist to make that possible.

All this means that the personal and professional obstacles that held people back are no longer as unmovable as before. If a person has mixed feelings about leaving India, if someone is unsure about how to use one's abilities best—in the U.S. where it may be easier from the standpoint of financial and transportation infrastructures or in India where help may be in greater need in some sectors—one can be in both places. You don't have to choose.

"I was born in Mumbai," says Shveta Raina, "and then went to Brown University as an undergraduate. A few years later I went to Harvard Business School where I got an M.B.A." Although her education was at two of the most elite schools on the planet, both in the Ivy League, Shveta maintained her focus, and did not *end up* joining or serving the elite. "I wanted to figure out India's biggest problems." Having the finest education prepared her for a career in consultancy, and she found work at the prestigious McKinsey & Company. "And then I launched my own business: Talerang. It's not an NGO, but rather it uses a social-enterprise based solution as a business model. We

With Ashok Advani (third from right), Founder Publisher of Business India Group, and other Talerang supporters.

Explaining how to create a vision board during a Talerang life visioning session.

select students from across India and prepare them for industry through a work-readiness programme."

But I stop Shveta here. Before she gets fully caught up in describing the extraordinary work she is doing *now*, I want to know: What brought you to the U.S. in the first place?

"I didn't like Indian education," she says simply. The requirement of that system to select a path for study at the very beginning of university that would lead to a vocation felt stifling. That educational model exists in the EU as well: students must choose at eighteen a course of study that is specific to future occupation. "I didn't know what I wanted to do," she confessed. "I felt creative *and* I was interested in math and science. In India you can't do both. And the main reason I wanted to go to Brown, in particular, is because of the Ivy League schools, it has the greatest opportunities for diversity in curriculum. You can try different courses, and through that openness see what you enjoy most and are best at doing."

Arriving at the age of seventeen, still a teenager, in Providence, Rhode Island must nonetheless, despite academic freedoms, been jarring. Brown recognized this and has a unique programme to help students to get acclimated.

"Brown has an international mentoring programme," Shveta explains, "as there are students at the university from all over the world." She laughs as she recalls its basics. "We started in this programme by recognizing a number of things." Such as? "Being open to the fact that everything in America is different, for one thing. It wasn't so much a way to teach us about the U.S. nor to know how we were doing. It was a programme to point out the differences. Such as, portion sizes! 'If you don't want to get fat, watch what you eat.'" The huge amounts of food served in many American restaurants is a bizarre sight for Europeans and Asians. "To get us sensitized to people wearing sweatpants to class. To the fact that many Americans shower more than once a day." To sensitive issues, too. "Sex education was part of the programme. How not to give someone the wrong idea. And so on."

Shveta had an advantage. The U.S. wasn't entirely new to her. "I had travelled to the States many, many times before Brown," she admits. "So it was less of a scare or transition for me. And as such, I became a mentor in the programme after completing it. We talked to a lot of concerned parents and reassured them. The parents had a lot of anxiety! Which they communicated in one way or another to their kids. So I and the other mentors would help with that, saying things like, 'There's nothing to be concerned about.'" She took what she had learned and applied it in far greater depth than just that one sentence to students who, as she had, needed help in adapting meaningfully to a new culture, a new set of rules.

Shveta's insight into the specifics of the many layers of how she and her fellow students were shaped by the uniqueness of each of their experiences is valuable. There is no formula for progress, no manual to read in order to be successful. But she does note certain factors she observed which made her think hard about what could help students from India fit in comfortably at Brown.

"There was a tendency for Indians to hang out with each other," she says, "and also a division between those people who had studied previously at one time or another in the U.S. and those who hadn't. So many Indians lived with other Indians. But I wanted to make friends from all over the world!"

The desire to mix it up intellectually was also—and remains so—part of Shveta's identity as a person. She had decided to come to Brown to be part of a new world while still committed to being who she was when she had arrived.

"I loved Brown," she says. "I had been dying to go away to college."

Then it was time at last to take what she had learned and apply it to real situations. That meant McKinsey, but before long she saw in India a place where her high-level skills were most needed.

"I wanted to come back," she says. "A major recession was going on in the U.S. It was 2009 and it felt as if the whole world was falling apart. On top of that, I wanted to make a difference in my country."

She returned to India to join Teach For India.

Through Teach For India, Shveta was able to make a direct impact. She left the Ivory tower of academia and the rarified atmosphere of McKinsey and returned to Mumbai. Goodbye academic and business elites, hello poverty.

"I had never been inside a slum," she says. "And there I found myself in Mumbai. The real India."

I admire her bravery and her commitment to making a change for those in need, but what did her family think? She had spent years and years in the Ivy League, and been hired by one of the world's leading consulting firms. And now she was back in India working to set up teaching programmes in low-income schools?

"What was my family's reaction?" She thinks about that for awhile before answering. "My parents thought I was making a big mistake: 'What is Teach For India? Is it like Teach For America?' There was no organization when I decided to take the job." The programme had just got started in June 2009. "But I have to say that I didn't think of what I was doing as an entire life decision. And yet: after doing it for two or two and a half years, I realized that I couldn't go back to a corporate job. Here I was leading the recruitment, marketing, and selection for a movement in education. Making a difference is addictive. You learn more. You feel better. And the feeling of being part of Teach for India was fantastic—it had a fantastic culture. I felt as if it was why I am here: life is short, make the most of it. I didn't feel financially insecure doing it. I never felt underpaid. I felt it was very fair."

From her education in the U.S. and her work there as well as in India, Shveta must have been faced with a fascinating and unusual set of challenges. And she did not want to have to choose one or the other. Her goal was to integrate knowledge and experience, and to cull the best and most useful from the range of what she had been taught and practiced.

All that led to Talerang. In the organization's written material, Talerang is described as having a, 'mission to develop work-ready graduates for India through a unique, experiential model researched as a project at Harvard Business School.' Further, 'Talerang began as a project at Harvard Business School with the aim to bridge the gap between what colleges teach and what organizations look for. After a year of conducting research at several organizations and running pilots at a few leading colleges in India, we found that less than sixty per cent of the students surveyed felt ready for a front-office job. Less than fifty per cent had someone to go to for advice on their life path. Almost fifty per cent of students at top undergraduate universities in India do not secure work internships in their college years, which makes their first job the first time they have ever worked.'

Lack of preparedness. Lack of mentoring. Lack of work experience. These are all areas of need that Talerang seeks to address.

But how does Shveta describe it in her *own* words?

"We launched in 2013," she says, "and currently what we do is run programmes to help prepare students to be work-ready. For example, we just did a programme where we trained about sixteen hundred people for over ten days with hundred and sixty to hundred and seventy-five students per class." She noted that about fifty per cent of the students in any given programme run by Talerang are provided with free involvement if they cannot afford the fees. "Basically," she continues, "we start with self awareness. What don't they want to do? Engineering? Humanities? It's almost a bit like group therapy."

People speaking openly and honestly about what they think, how they feel, and what they want to do with their lives. How to get there. Not just following a path set for them by parents or caste. Not exactly typical for India, is it?

"They share life journeys," Shveta says. "Opening up in an American way. Which is indeed very foreign to India, very alien, in fact. They open up and truly discover who they are. They identify their values and acknowledge their fears. And then we transition to life vision: professionally and personally. After which we work on communication skills." Shveta confides: "Indians work hard, but not creatively." She's not being judgmental, but rather observing that versatility in thinking is not as key a component in India as it is in the U.S.

From the abstract realms of insight, synthetic thinking, and visionary ideals, Shveta makes note of very practical considerations deemed necessary for advancement.

"There are some real facts we teach as well," she says. "The need to shower. To brush one's hair. And so on. Students at engineering colleges were telling us at the outset that they were using a deodorant once in three days. That's not enough. We found that the average student at some engineering colleges takes a shower once every two days."

Having identified strengths and goals, and literally cleaned up their acts, what is the final step in getting people ready for work?

"The last module is teaching students how to write resumes, use Excel, do a PowerPoint presentation, network, and conduct oneself in a job interview," Shveta explains. We do this over sixty hours, and we have a hybrid model with omnichannel training (online and offline components).

The combination of cultural values from two cultures seems to be a seamless amalgam, but clearly Shveta has put an enormous amount of thought into creating a new organization with deep originality. It didn't happen overnight, there was no blueprint to follow.

"A lot is based on Year UP," she says modestly. "As well as from Teach For America, which Teach For India is based on. My thought is that there is a lack of exposure to skills in India needed to be ready for work, and that the lack can lead to a lack of confidence and poor communication. In the U.S. there is more general education, and it's a richer country, so there can be a lot to learn from the West. But there is learning in both directions. From India, in my personal experience, self awareness is special. We have here a culture that is influenced by Gandhian philosophy, by which I mean: simplicity, bonding, humility. It's not about bringing change, but *being the change.*"

The back and forth from India to the States, and not just the U.S. but its elite educational system, nonetheless must take place within an already existing corporate structure in India. Those corporations have their own way of doing things, their traditions, biases, and plans. Talerang, the remarkable organization that Shveta founded from scratch, prepares young Indians for work, but are corporate employers in India prepared for *them?*

"A lot of the companies I work with don't hire undergraduates historically," Shveta says, "but what we've done is changing that. They have started hiring graduates as interns, and this idea of internships, which is new to India, is part of the change. We're trying to change corporate attitudes. Then the best students will stay in India. Today over hundred companies recruit undergraduates, mainly from Talerang!"

Because then they see a future that is neither Indian nor American, but the best of both, a true hybrid, a new future without borders.

THE CHALLENGES
OF TODAY
Smitha Radhakrishnan _____

The more I hear the inspiring stories of great achievers in the Indian diaspora, the more I wonder: how is it possible? No other immigrant group to the United States has achieved so much in so many fields in so short a time. The narratives each person provides are riveting: supportive families, new arrivals who never gave up, great versatility in thinking, the excitement of living in a country where one's accent, region, gender, and social status are not quite as limiting as in India.

When Americans who are not from India meet Indians, they don't wonder: What caste is he? What language does she speak at home? What is his religion? For Americans, the person is simply Indian. Judged as foreign perhaps, misunderstood culturally, but with a completely different set of standards, ideas, and preconceptions than back home.

There is great freedom in not being confined to a set of prejudices (or at least a different set). But that doesn't explain the remarkable achievement, it only contextualizes it. What else can we understand about the patterns of immigration from India to the United States to help us understand better how it happened?

Indians born in the United States contribute to our understanding of the phenomenon. The first couple of waves of Indian immigrants, prior to the change in Civil Rights legislation of the 1960s as well as those who came over following the State of Emergency in the 1980s, and after, produced children passionately curious about their culture, as it exists in diaspora.

Academically affiliated at major U.S. universities, scholars who are Indian provide essential knowledge.

Smitha Radhakrishnan notes that her expertise is in 'gender, globalization, and development.' A tenured faculty member at Wellesley College, an all-women's institution (which is Hilary Clinton's alma mater) set on sprawling, bucolic grounds just outside of Boston, Smitha is thorough in her analysis.

"We have to look at the context of migration," she says. "Such that in 1965 there was a selection of Indians allowed in. Specifically, only 'smart ones' were let in.'"

Smitha refers to the law that Asian immigrants were only permitted in both by a fixed quota and a law that required them to have university education. This implicitly racist policy, which was not applied to Western immigrants from Europe, kept out people who had a range of non-academic skills. Applied to India, where access to higher education was historically denied to those without privilege, it meant that the elite in India could arrive *as an elite* to the United States. Unlike other immigrants from other nations, Indians who immigrated during the period of quotas and requirements, already had in place a deep sophistication about how to convey ideas, manage people, plan finances, and negotiate from a position of strength. Ironically, their early success, which was nearly a foregone conclusion given their advantages, paved the way for the next waves of immigrants who did not have their privileges.

The early immigrants not only created social networks, they established social acceptance. Indians were usually accepted in the United States despite their foreignness in clothing, style, ways of speaking, differences of religion, and so on. The elite who came here compensated for all that through deep intellectual and social sophistication. Accustomed to a certain status at home, they expected the same in the U.S., and acted accordingly. They may have been new arrivals, but they weren't new to being the upper crust. The fact that they were met by respect, in general, meant that subsequent arrivals would benefit.

It is unusual in any country for foreigners to be accepted as readily and as broadly as the early Indian immigrants were in the United States in the 1960s. Most people at that time had little personal contact with Indians, but cultural artefacts stemming from India garnered interest. Even if many of these were stereotypes and cartoonish, at least they were positive: sitar music, colourful Hindu gods, Nehru jackets, spicy food, yoga, meditation, etc. The images suggested a society or nation invested in spiritual betterment. While the early immigrants were chiefly scientists and engineers, who were far more intellectual than offbeat, what North Americans *understood* of India was peace and love.

We have The Beatles to thank for that.

But pop culture aside, the most powerful and influential of all is Mahatma Gandhi. He is so important a figure in the consciousness of North Americans that on the standardized

I.Q. test for adults there is even a question about him: Who was Mahatma Gandhi? It is a sign of intelligence, according to the scoring system in the test manual, to know who Gandhi was.

Gandhi is shorthand for all the things that India and America have in common, and chiefly it is three critical matters.

First, both nations kicked out the British. Afterwards, India and the U.S. established democracies. The two nations stood out in their regions as places where institutions, though very imperfect, exist to offer ordinary citizens opportunities for free speech and access to power.

Second, both nations are multicultural and multi-linguistic, but have one shared language: English. The immigrants who arrive here know how to navigate easily. It is like being at home in that sense.

And, finally, it was Gandhi whose ideas and courage, related to a philosophy of non-violence, inspired Americans, led by Martin Luther King, Jr., to work towards transforming a racist society into one that is based on respect and merit through legislative action that would guarantee civil rights for everyone.

All this created a climate of progress in which the generations of Indians born here, or who arrived in more recent decades, could take things to the next level.

Smitha, born and raised in Phoenix, Arizona, benefited from the achievements that preceded. Now she is conducting research meant to address societal ills that were left ignored previously. Without the previous success of those who arrived long ago, her work would not be possible.

Her research focuses on the micro-finance industry. Small banks that provide critical funding in the developing world, and insofar as she teaches classes on the role of gender and identity, some of Smitha's work focuses on the small banks that help empower women financially.

Her work looks at a huge variety of structures within India. The poorest women do not qualify for loans, but working class women are eligible for support.

"You see working class women in slums working two or three jobs," she says, "to earn money needed to pay school fees, or to make repairs for homes as basic as new roofs."

These women can get involved in training programmes designed to help them be entrepreneurs.

"The purpose of these programmes is to create financial literacy," she says.

With knowledge and skills of money management, the goal is to learn how to budget, save money, sort out what opportunities are of greatest financial benefit, and take charge of one's economic future.

It's a kind of gender global politics, as she describes it, with women achieving independence through control of their incomes.

The context for Smitha's philosophy is the world-as-it-stands, which means that there is a framework of so-called 'tech superiority.'

"Tech superiority," she explains, "refers to my first project about transnational Indians in IT, not my current project on microfinance."

Where do women fit in that world? What is the broad role of women within tech?

"What I end up arguing," Smitha says, "is that a lot of that image of tech superiority is underpinned by women working at home."

In other words, women create a domestic stability that allows men to dominate tech. That varies from one country to the next. What is expected of a woman and possible for them depends on whether or not she is in India or the U.S. But enough is the same in both countries such that women do not have the same mobility as men in tech in either place.

Hence, at a basic level, providing women with entrepreneurial skills will prepare them for future independence at home.

What's fascinating about Smitha's work and progress is how she builds on the ideas of generations that came before her. She brings the past into the future.

In that way, it is clear and exciting to see the relevance of Indian civic mindedness take on new meaning as it is applied to strengthening women's role in society.

"What do you do to mobilize at any moment?" she asks, rhetorically.

HARVARD, YALE, HEALTH COMMISSIONER FOR NEW YORK STATE, COO FOR THE KAISER FOUNDATION
Dr. Nirav R. Shah

He is only forty-three years old, but Dr. Nirav R. Shah has accumulated a lifetime of experience and established a deep well of knowledge. On top of being profoundly intelligent and a physician who focuses on public health, Dr. Shah has demonstrated leadership. This all comes at a time of what many consider to be a crisis in American medicine. As resources become scarce due to increased access to medical care, and as the profession itself becomes increasingly monetized, the role of a public sector doctor has great importance. Dr. Shah is a leader in the field. He is now based in Pasadena, California.

How did it all happen?

"I grew up in Buffalo, New York," Nirav says. Buffalo is upstate, notorious for long, freezing winters with lots of snow. As a second generation Indian, whose parents were born in India, he had the advantage of living in two cultures. The one outside the home was all-American. The one inside the home was all-Indian. At once it is apparent that the division between private sector and public sector was never abstract for him. He must have understood, even before there were words to describe it at the time, how private matters and life in the community could be and often were radically different. This had to have some influence on his thinking. For even without growing up in a geographical India, he lived in an Indian home. "We had a large extended family. The diet stayed vegetarian. And while India progressed over the decades, my parents raised me in the culture they left—of India in the 1960s."

Growing up in what was in many ways a traditional home, foreign in its habits and philosophies, could have been an alienating experience. But it was much more of an addition to what Nirav saw as a child and teenager, and a perspective or lens through which to observe and analyze the broader culture.

"Buffalo in the 1970s still had a somewhat 1950s or 1960s organization of family," he says, and then laughs, before adding: "A bit like *The Brady Bunch*." He is referencing a famous American T.V. show from the late 1960s to mid-1970s about a white suburban family in which social issues were relegated to day-to-day pleasantries. It was as if the family was on Mars while on Earth the Vietnam war was raging, there was civil

With wife Nidhi Shah and their kids at Yosemite National Park, 2015.

unrest in cites, and racism was in full throttle. "It was a time of very nuclear families in America," Nirav continues. "It seemed to me that the importance of community as a whole had lost focus. I try in my work, I always have tried, to capture elements of community. There is resilience that comes from community, and it doesn't have to be culture specific, per se. Look, in the U.S., sports and work bring people together, but those activities do not provide the same sense of community."

I'm fascinated by Nirav's ability to formulate what are essentially personal experiences inculcated through a bicultural life. He takes the real and imaginative experiences of his childhood and adolescence and brings them to life not just through his words, but also his actions. Sometimes this is how greatness occurs and develops: an individual takes what happened to them, or what they participated in, and creates a global point of view. For an Indian growing up among Indians, with a keen awareness of the differences between what he was taught at home and what he learned among Americans, the opportunity for growth must have been profound. He also found concordance among other communities in Buffalo, New York, whose values struck a chord.

"The Jewish families I got to know were like ours," he says. "With an emphasis on education and community. It seemed to be especially true in Buffalo. I think our suburb had a population that was about one-third Jewish, so many of my friends were Jewish and my cohorts—their families resembled my own. The focus on education was clear!"

Nirav contrasts the importance that education had in his household, and in the homes of his Jewish friends, with other concerns that are more typically American. The country, as a whole, seeks to flatten experience, to create activities that cross ethnicities, races, religions, classes, and nationalities. In this way, through shared participation or observation, a sense of community grows. One can more or less place one's ethnic, racial, religious, class, or national identity within another context. While the new experience is frankly superficial, it can alleviate the tensions and spiralling hatreds which divide people. It's the American way, and what we are talking about here?

Sports!

Sports are the parameter for an American child and teenager: watching, playing, talking about favourite football, basketball, or baseball players as if they are demi-gods. Never mind the books. Never mind the intellectual curiosity. Never mind the cultivation of an inner, emotional life that is often the impetus for change.

"But my parents could care less about sports," Nirav says. "It was nothing like most other Americans."

I wonder about his parents. Now in their early seventies.

"My folks were the cream of the crop," Nirav says. "Kind of like frontier people." He refers to the fact that they were part of an early generation of immigrants who arrived without knowing many people in a country where there were not many Indians at a time when being foreign had a different set of connotations than it does today. "They were the only vegetarians in town.

The only Indians in a sea of white faces. And they had very different expectations."

Back then it must have been a time of focus on what was immediately possible and, just as critical, what needed to be done so that Nirav's generation could succeed in a new country. The second generation's paramount challenges—assimilation, participation in civic institutions, integration into an 'American way of life' while holding onto what makes a person Indian, contributing Indian ideas and ways of doing things to the overall culture—were not on the table. It was in many ways the classic conundrum of many immigrant groups in the U.S.: facing up to day-to-day discrimination, sacrificing for one's children's future, and preserving the past. It is a tall order.

"Growing up," Nirav recalls, "we went to temple every weekend. We celebrated Diwali. My parents' friends were Indian. And as an Indian community, our parents only focused on how well we did in school. I was also very lucky to have grandparents who were very involved in my life, from Bombay. They would visit us frequently, and we stayed very connected." He pauses. "My maternal grandparents were very wealthy. They had gone on a world tour, and they wanted their kids to marry spouses who would eventually settle in America." Which, of course, is unusual. So the gallivanting, the desire to get out and push forward started two generations back! "My mom didn't want to go, but my father did. He got an M.A. and Ph.D. at Stanford and wanted to return to the U.S."

Ensconced in America, Nirav's parents made a new life, and one that was complex in its internal richness of ideas and diversity of expression. Eager to be in a new world and still immersed in the world they had come from.

"There were so many opportunities in America," says Nirav. Even then. "The educational system, for example, was such that one could learn about several fields of study. Had they stayed in India, it would have been a narrow focus on one field. Here one had the promise of 'The American Dream.' And what happened was that all of my mother's siblings, two sisters and two brothers, all came in turn." He tells of his father's brother, not speaking English, who his father sponsored, and who went to Alfred University, in upstate New York, eventually becoming a military contractor.

So with a background of wealthy grandparents in India and growing up in a home with heritage, along with his own success at Harvard and Yale, how does Nirav shape his identity as an Indian? What does he give up? What does he hold onto?

"The Indian kids of my generation? We pick and choose," he says. "We have the best of both cultures. From the U.S., we had education. From India, we have the diligence, sense of community, and persistence of our elders."

In retrospect, Nirav's path to public health—he was the Health Commissioner for New York State from 2011 to 2014, and his work was frequently the subject of articles in *The New York Times*—seems an obvious path, but what were the necessary steps he took to get there?

"I was an academic," he says. "At UCLA. Then I went to New York City where I practiced medicine one day a week and conducted research the other four days. But after six or seven years, I got bored with just getting grants and publishing papers. I was looking for other things to do and have a greater impact, and spent a lot of time consulting. One of the people I wound up meeting was Governor Andrew Cuomo. He and his inner circle asked me to help select the next health commissioner for the state. After a week, forty-four people applied." He smiles. "I was an Indian American doctor with a degree in Internal Medicine practicing primary care at Bellevue Hospital." He still sounds amazed though it is years later. "I was only thirty-eight years old." He laughs. "I thought I was too young to have enemies. I had no reputation. But the governor offered me the job."

His humility is genuine, but Nirav was, in fact, well qualified for the position. With an undergraduate degree from Harvard and an M.D.-M.P.H. (Masters in Public Health) from Yale. On top of that, the impression is that from an early age he understood intuitively the importance of public life as differentiated from private life. Moreover, his background, with a family from India where public health problems are huge, had a bearing upon his outlook and passion.

"I asked myself: 'How do we optimize health, not just maximize healthcare delivery?' I thought about public health issues in India. Although Yale wouldn't let me explore this fully, it was on my mind. I realized that India made vast gains through the agricultural revolution, but that there was a large gap in health care. Growing up and seeing poverty during annual visits to India, I learned that the goal has to be to invest in healthy communities."

Nirav's work in New York inspired him to continue his leadership and explorations in U.S. medicine. Now at Kaiser Permanente in Southern California, he is the Chief Operating Officer of a $24B health system with over four million members. Hospital quality, use of technology, better patient outcomes, medical education, research. Comprehensively, his job is all about the integration of public *and* private medical care aimed at efficiency and best use of resources for those in need.

One gets the sense that Nirav is really at the beginning of his career despite all that he has achieved up until now. Given his youth, and that there is so much to learn. But more than that, his unique background—growing up in two very different cultures—has provided him with a great deal to weave together and apply globally to all sorts of situations. That he knows two cultures intimately gives him flexibility in how he thinks and responds to medical and personal challenges. And naturally he continues to put India into the foreground.

"At one time," he says, "I tried to set up low-cost primary care clinics in the suburbs of Mumbai." What happened? "I gave that up when I became health commissioner."

What's in store for tomorrow?

CHANGING THE WORLD THROUGH PUBLIC POLICY
Pradeep Nair

When you consider the astronomical profits, the sums of money, to be made in the private sector, whether in finance or IT, what motivates a person to devote his or her life to help create a public sector? An infrastructure that will benefit all or most, a sense that societies, which work to diminish suffering and include the weakest, are the ones that have the most depth and integrity. This altruism, fuelled by empathy, isn't easy to come by. And reaching the point where these things matter is not a trajectory one can follow like a business plan.

Pradeep Nair is currently the director of the Performance, Impact and Innovation Programme of the Volcker Alliance, a hugely influential and global foundation. Started in 2013 by Paul Volcker, former Federal Reserve Board Chairman, the foundation aims 'to address the challenge of effective execution of public policies and to help rebuild public trust in government.' Prior to this, Pradeep worked for the Institute for Sustainable Communities, helping to launch their India office. And prior to that, he was director of the Clinton Foundation, started by the President, 'designing and expanding their global programmes, managing India strategy and operations and later helping to establish the C40 Cities group in the South Asia region.' But how did he get there? What about being Indian led him on this career path in public policy?

"I grew up in Kuwait," Pradeep begins. "My father had been working there as an engineer, and continued with higher education in India. He instilled in me the need to be an engineer. And then I got an M.B.A. But you know what? Indians are realizing that there are more professions! And I have to tell you something else." He laughs. "My real passion, what I inherited from my mother, is cooking. I didn't learn it from her. I mean, the way I cook? I improvise."

After living and working in Germany for two years, Pradeep came to the U.S. The year was 1999. What led him to make the move? He makes it all sound so down-to-earth, and indeed his appreciation for the simple pleasures of life, whether cooking or being open to experience, seems to characterize him.

Having a grand time snowboarding.

"There was a technology opportunity in California," he shares. "I thought California sounded like a nice place. It was meant to be a short assignment."

But it is often the 'short' assignments, the surprises, the vicissitudes or successes, which can transform someone *if* that person is willing to accept change. Had he stayed in Kuwait or India, Pradeep probably would have become a fine engineer or business person. But coming to California, like many others who for over a century have arrived in that strange and innovative state, changed him and the direction of his life.

"It sounded like a fun opportunity," Pradeep says. "It was the early days of the Internet. I thought: I'll have fun. So one thing led to another. And I became an American citizen. And now when I think of the question 'Where are you from?' as it pertains to me, I never know. Well," he laughs, "I like saying *Indian*. But I must say that I also like the feeling of belonging to more than one place." His sense of fitting in means that who he is in private is balanced very much by how he *feels* in public. He is very much a person at home in public and private spaces, cognizant of society and a keen observer of the critical importance of those around us, and how they live, in shaping the dimensions of our personalities. "I'm now in New York City. Since last year." The pleasure he takes in adaptability is compelling. "Now I think of myself as a New Yorker. My window to get adjusted is very short. Are there downsides? Sure. When friends talk about continuous memories they have of a place, I don't have that. Nor does my wife; she grew up in the Middle East." He pauses thoughtfully. For all his enthusiasm and youthful vigour, Pradeep remains at his core a deep thinker. "I feel like I become myself everywhere. I don't have a strong attachment to one place."

His ability to shift cultural attitudes stems from moving around a lot in his youth, and it is enhanced by his love of that experience. Had he been the sort of person who found it distasteful to be uprooted or someone who was wed to what he was taught as a boy, he might be unhappy. Instead, Pradeep embraces the richness of surrender and amalgamation—he gives up iconic values, he adds iconic values. Who he becomes as an individual is Indian *and* it is American; who he is as a leader in developing public infrastructure is informed by his altruism *and* his business sense.

"Personal and social diversity affected my professional life," says Pradeep. "It helped tremendously. I just relate to people immediately. I can readily understand others. Because I've been exposed to so many types of people—that helps!" He feels very fortunate. "Very few people have my exposure to so many communities." His delight in diversity is remarkable. Rather than bring forward stereotypes of other cultures or cling to some unfounded, grossly sentimental and divisive notions of one culture being better than another, Pradeep recognizes that so much of what separates people and impedes progress are artificial constructs. "Most of my relationships have been brokering ties. All of my organizations are based on that." Again, the simplicity of the explanation skims the profound depth of his understanding. Pradeep is good at getting to the crux of what makes things work, what makes a solution viable. "In the

U.S., and most western countries, any professional relationship between strangers starts with trust. Having a meeting? You are building trust. Or trying. Because of course it might end with distrust. It's different in Asia, in my experience. There it starts with distrust. You sell yourself, not the product!"

Living and working in Kuwait, India, and the U.S. with an open mind and a keen intellect provided Pradeep with an array of possibilities, culturally and professionally. His observation about trust, for example, is a valuable insight into a psychological state that has economic purpose. Hence, he synthesizes not only culture, but ways of thinking: economy, psychology, culture. All these things seemingly disparate are, in fact, tied together.

"I'm a relationship driven person," Pradeep continues. "Just being Indian in the U.S. has reinforced that. And because I grew up in the Middle East, and live here now, I'm not completely accepted in India. But I'm not completely Indian American either." He smiles, then. "I fall into that group: Global citizen."

Pradeep's knowledge, focus, and global experience caught the attention of former President Bill Clinton. President Clinton hired him to run his foundation from 2008 to 2012.

"I set up operations in India," Pradeep tells. "Climate work. Climate programmes. Localizing in different regions. And federal as well as state. We worked, for example, on localized solutions and on decentralization."

That work led to his current position.

"Which is fantastic," he says, "though my wife and kids are still in Mumbai for the moment." They will join him shortly.

Through the Volcker Alliance, Pradeep takes what were ideas germinated in India and applies some of these, as well as strategies he implemented there, on a global scale. These are moves that can literally change the world in every sense.

"It was public sector," Pradeep says, the excitement in his voice changing its tenor. "I had a vision." Which others shared. "I come from a very unique caste," he continues. "My last name is Nair, as you know. And my caste is matrilineal. The decision-maker is a woman. If you don't have a girl, your family doesn't go on. This has always been very refreshing for me. It was like, 'Wait a minute. Why does the entire world want boys?'" He laughs. "I was exposed to this social organization as a child. You could even say since I was a baby. My grandmother and mother knew everyone in town. They had relationships." These relationships made it abundantly clear that what mattered most were ties—between people who shared common interests and needs, but who might not have the same social background. It was a quiet ideology. "My mother and grandmother," Pradeep says wistfully, "invested in getting to know people." That had an enormous impact on him, and serves to this day as his most visceral sense of home—not a nation, caste, or gender. But instead what sustains him are his grandmother and mother, and their love of the public sector: who they met each day. "I genuinely love to get to know people," he says.

And given his unusual upbringing and peripatetic life, what might he suggest to others who have more conventional backgrounds? Is his life story simply to be admired? Or are there lessons to learn?

"My advice is to build your own experiences," Pradeep says cheerfully. His positive outlook must have always been there, a fundament of how willing he is to experience life, which means to be changed by it. "Be completely open. Don't come to the U.S. with too much mental baggage. Know what to let go of and what to hold on to. Some ills exist in a society which is really old. But it cannot be all wrong. And then, too, ask yourself, 'What is culture?' No one has been able to explain it to me."

THE PUBLIC SECTOR, THE PRIVATE SECTOR

Kapil Sharma

With economic gains, greater integration, and broad acceptance, it's natural that members of the Indian American community have entered the U.S. political arena. Going back and forth from private sector to public sector is intrinsic to that process. There are the men and women in the limelight, and then, too, people behind the scenes who forge connections, delineate agendas, and turn ideals into realities.

"I'm not the very famous comedian," says Kapil Sharma, with a laugh. He shares the name of a well-known performer. "I'm a lawyer."

Formerly a prominent staffer on Capitol Hill, Kapil now is the Senior General Manager for the vast and powerful Tata group in their North American operations. As Tata's chief representative, he works closely with the corporation in its dealings with federal, state, and local governments in the U.S. I caught up with him and he took time out from his frenetic schedule in New Jersey to talk about the success of Indians in America. Kapil has a terrific perspective since he works in the world of Indian industry as well as in the public and private sectors of the United States. Few people know as much as him when it comes to figuring out the differences and similarities between so many places.

"I honestly think that language is a big part of the Indian success in the U.S.," he says. "English has been a part of life in India for quite some time, after all. Compare this to the immigrant groups from Korea or China. The initial arrivals were not as comfortable with English. There is a great bridge between India and the U.S. due to sharing a common language."

Kapil—who was born in the U.K., but came with his parents to the U.S. at six months old and then grew up in Eatontown, Monmouth County—was also exposed to diverse groups of people in New Jersey, which added to his understanding of and appreciation for not only Indian culture, but that of other nations' as well. He went on to Rutgers, the state university, where his education was both cultural and academic. He was learning more and more how to work and live in several cultures simultaneously.

"I call myself a second-generation Indian," he says. "My father is a retired teacher, my mother a nurse."

While at college, Kapil found himself in two communities with as much internal diversity as external. After all, the Americans he met, the non-Indians, were from many different cultures and the Indians he spent time with had very different backgrounds.

"I never really identified myself as Indian American at college," he confesses. "I couldn't relate to Indian American girls, for example. But more broadly I see that time in my life as a phase of self discovery." He laughs self-deprecatingly. "I was kind of what we called a Twinkie or a coconut or a potato—dark on the outside, white on the inside."

As he matured emotionally, got his law degree, and better understood the richness of being at home in more than one culture, Kapil became more political. Both about the unique situation of Indians in America as well as the field of politics itself.

"A whole world was opening for me," he says. "It was around the 1990s, and the Indian Caucus had formed on Capitol Hill. This was in response, in part, to the notorious Dotbusters."

Kapil refers to the racially-motivated hate crimes perpetrated on Indians, who were identified by their bindis. Stemming from these attacks, the first hate crime laws were passed in the U.S, but not before people's lives were destroyed. These events were a turning point in his life, and he became an activist.

Due to the attention being paid to his work in the state where hate crimes were taking place, Kapil was invited to the White House. And from that point, he became closely involved with the Indian Caucus. He discovered that, ironically, despite the fact that it was a community that also faced hatred and discrimination, opposition to the goals of the Indian Caucus came from the Black Caucus.

"What had happened was this," he explains. "When inner cities had riots and unrest, such as after the Rodney King beating in Los Angeles, the Korean shopkeepers moved out and were replaced by Indians. This meant that the poor could focus their dissatisfaction on the Indian community, and when the Indian Caucus sought congressional support, the Black Caucus fought it and gave into pressure from local leaders."

During his time in politics, Kapil was senior counsel and legislative director to N.J.'s Senator Robert Torricelli and then worked as a legislative assistant to Congressman Frank Pallone.

Kapil expresses disappointment in the divide between both the political parties as well as the two communities—black and Indian—that actually have more in common than not. His sense that the Democrats were unresponsive to the needs of Indians led him to switch allegiance to the Republican Party. Ostensibly, this is an unusual move since historically it has always been the Democratic Party that promoted and pushed forward immigration and civil rights legislation of the most benefit to Indians.

Kapil sounds very cynical as he speaks of the divisions and changes and compromises that are fundamental to politics, and it may be that this cynicism helped spur his decision to enter the private sector. He speaks admiringly of Gandhi and Martin Luther King, Jr., but the situation on the ground was anything but idealistic. Sometimes when ideals are implemented, the person practicing ways to bring people together can feel that his or her values are lost in the shuffle. It wasn't as if Kapil was in charge of an N.G.O. or the leader of an independent organization where he had control. He had to work with many different groups, of varying power, and surely the opportunity to build a broad consensus for positive change must have been extremely frustrating.

Leaving politics then for the private sector, Kapil joined up with Tata, and from 2008 through 2011 he lived and worked in Mumbai. What was it like for a young man from New Jersey to be in the country his parents had left to start a new life?

"There were big challenges for me working in India," he says. "On a personal level, my wife, who has an M.A. in International Relations from George Washington University, could only get limited employment. But there were also cultural issues."

Having grown up in the States meant that Kapil had gotten used to operating within the American way of doing business and socializing. While evidently Indian, he was as much a guy from New Jersey as he was someone whose family history originated in India.

"There were three main challenges I faced in Mumbai," he says with a laugh. "There was the matter of language—nuances, regional differences. Questions—in the States, questions are a routine part of a business discussion or a conversation. Whereas I found in Mumbai that I wasn't supposed to ask so many questions, it wasn't considered appropriate culturally." He pauses, then laughs some more before finally listing the third challenge. "And finally there was the matter of sarcasm. People can joke in the States quite often. Not in Mumbai. I got in a little trouble for that!"

And yet there were deep commonalities beneath the surface of behavioural and cultural differences. The differences in how people acted could be improved through shared affiliation. It's fascinating to hear Kapil speak of what enabled him to fit in and ultimately feel at home in Mumbai. In a fundamental way, Kapil answered, at least for himself (and with broader implications for many other Indians in the diaspora), the fundamental question: What does it mean to be Indian?

"We share a rich cultural heritage," he says. He refers then to specific philosophies and approaches to life. "Family. Almost every Indian I know has strong ties to family, which includes respect for elders. If someone is older than me, I defer to that person as a sign of respect. And there's also something thought of as 'the nod.' You see something similar in the African-American community. A nod from one Indian to another in a setting where there may be few of us is a sign that we are together." That solidarity extends to the community, at home and abroad, as a whole.

We talk more about the features of Indian identity, both in the U.S. and in India, and the subject turns to the centrality of education.

"The conversation that we're all having among ourselves as second-generation Indian Americans is concerned in part about future education," he says. "Our parents worked hard— good colleges, good jobs. I'm not sure if *our* kids have the same outlook, I don't know if the drive towards education is cultural or not. I mean, kids are bombarded with other things in the U.S.; they are not out of villages. For the generation before mine, education was the only way out. It's what brought them to the U.S."

The respect and appreciation for the sacrifices of the previous generation raises challenges, too. Now that the previous generation is getting older, what will be the responsibilities of their children? In India, it is often expected that older family members will move in with their adult children. What about in the U.S.? Talk about cultural differences!

"Absolutely," agrees Kapil. "We ask ourselves: 'Will we have the ability to take care of our parents? Can we afford it? How do we do it? And if one doesn't help 'enough,' then one becomes a pariah in the Indian community. After all, we were all raised to be dutiful kids!"

Kapil notes that taking care of elderly parents is problematic in India, too. With increased mobility and affluence, parents can be 'abandoned' there as well.

The irony of Kapil's biculturalism is remarkable. Both Indian and American, with unique vantage points to observe the cultures in each nation, he can select so many different solutions or strategies for problem solving. But narrowing down choices can be difficult.

"I have a lot of Indian friends in the U.S.," he says. "Indians born in India who came to the States. And there are pressures at times placed on my wife and me to adopt their more traditional ways of doing things. Like sociability. Indians, in my experience, tend to be more social than their counterparts in the U.S. For example, we like to get together with other couples, but not *every* Friday or *every* Saturday. We're not like that."

And, finally, there is the matter of what Kapil will imbue in his children. They, too, will have the luxury of a multi-faceted identity, but theirs will differ from his.

"It's a lot different for them," he says wistfully. "Disciplining kids here is a lot harder than in India, for example. I saw kids run wild in restaurants there, and when we don't allow that sort of thing, friends and family from India when visiting will ask, 'Why doesn't America like kids?'"

WE CONCLUDE
OUR TRIP FOR
NOW WITH
EDUCATORS,
THE NEXT
GENERATION,
A PSYCHOLOGIST,
MEDIA GENIUSES,
THE MAN FROM
PHILADELPHIA,
AND A SONG
FOR TOMORROW

WHAT HAVE WE LEARNED?
Maya Ajmera

Assimilation into the U.S. culture and society was the goal of many Indian families. They wanted their children to fit in. Fitting in meant feeling comfortable at home and in school, and it ensured that the opportunity to lead and be part of a group of fellow Americans would be there. It wasn't always possible.

There was often the stigma of being an outsider, whether through skin colour, religion, accent, style of dress, attachment to values that were unfamiliar to neighbours, ways of cooking, and social behaviours across the spectrum of what passes for civility in the U.S.

There were also occupational barriers. Before 1980, Indians were seen as engineers or tech people, and were not evident in big numbers in the full array of professions.

Now that all that has changed, a new puzzle has emerged: How do families keep their Indian-ness? What does it mean to be Indian?

One important characteristic worth speculating about is the role of empathy in Indian societies. Unlike the U.S. where poverty is sequestered often in segregated cities and neighbourhoods, India is a hodgepodge of rich and poor.

In the United States, where do upper middle class families encounter people from the unemployed classes? Chiefly through the media, in public parks, in supermarkets, and in pharmacies. But the actual, real human contact isn't there. That's not the case in India.

In India, with few exceptions, the contact between the entitled and the impoverished is part of everyday life. Even as the limos wind their way through the slum streets, passengers from the cool, mirrored interiors can see the faces of those who have nothing. In the homes of those who luxuriate, staffs, who subsist, provide routine, hourly service and live day-to-day. The contact is physical. And while it's possible to become inured to empathizing with those who endure the pain of living without

confidence in a future, at the very least there exists in the entitled, at an unconscious level, some true awareness of The Other. That visualization leads invariably to an emotional response that may not stay buried, and can lead instead to social activism.

And even with a transplant to the United States, that sense of justice and caring remains incubated. Assimilation takes place within personalities of individuals who have not forgotten what is like to know those who have been denied basic human rights. What's remarkable, therefore, is that a unique platform has arisen. Combined with an historical sense of inequality, there is in the U.S. the entrepreneurial chance to actually create widespread movements to help the poor. Being both Indian and American creates a whole new way of seeing and doing things.

Maya Ajmera—born in Iowa City, Iowa, America's heartland, and raised from the age of three in eastern North Carolina in a small university town, Greenville—grew up in an Indian American household. She lives now in the Washington, D.C. Her father had a doctorate in electrical engineering, and science was a huge part of family discussions. What made her unique was that, in addition to adopting American life, she visited India frequently while growing up.

"I saw the haves and have-nots," she says.

Maya later travelled through Southeast and South Asia as a young woman, independently, and although she describes her parents being worried about her safety, she travelled from Thailand to Pakistan. It was while on the road that Maya had a life-changing experience—her moment of obligation.

"It was in March 1990," she recalls, "and I was in Bhubaneshwar in the state of Odisha, or formerly called Orissa, at a train platform, and it was very chaotic. I saw fifty kids and they were learning how to read and write. I speak Hindi, but I didn't speak their local language of Oriya. A teacher who was teaching at the train platform told me that the children slept, ate, played on the train platform and did not go to school. The school was brought to the train platform. I asked how much does it cost to run a platform school. She said, $400 a year to educate fifty kids and provide a meal everyday!"

And do something she did. With the drive and idealism of a twenty-two-year old, Maya had her moment of obligation to help the most impoverished children in the world.

"It seemed very simple at that age," she says, with a laugh. "The idea was to establish an organization that would invest small amounts of capital in innovative grassroots organizations and help them scale and build sustainability. I would also found a children's book publishing venture to teach children the similarities we all share."

As she speaks, there is magic to what she is saying because it's possible to see the schools beside the train tracks. Kids with books, kids who begin to use the power of language to express their ideas and observations. Kids who can see worlds in books that are utterly different from their daily lives, and in the course of that rich, imaginative experience to begin perhaps to see a way out of crushing poverty.

"What ended up happening to me personally," Maya continues, "was that although I had planned a traditional route of going to medical school that I decided to put it off."

Instead, Maya founded in 1993 what became one of the world's most famous nonprofits dedicated to bettering the lives of children existing in poverty around the globe: The Global Fund for Children. She took the experience of being Indian and aware of marginalized communities, and combined that with the can-do mentality of an American.

"We started The Global Fund for Children with seed money of $25,000 from Echoing Green, a social venture capital fund," she said. Nowadays, The Global Fund for Children has millions of dollars and millions of readers around the world and thousands of donors.

The emotional challenge of foregoing a traditional path of medical school and choosing instead to better the world through educating children meant being resilient enough to believe in her core values and answer the legitimate questions raised by her concerned parents.

"It may have been difficult for my parents to understand," she says. "My father came to this country with $500 and his suitcase. He was highly trained, and very good at negotiating ambiguity. My father was part of the generation in the 1960s that were professionals in the field of science."

But there was something else about her parents that shaped them as people. Her mother and father are Jains, and the concepts and philosophy of Jainism had obvious bearing upon their outlook on life. Although Maya did not marry within the Jain community—her husband is Jewish—she acknowledges that the family values she was brought up with are similar to those of her spouse. So it must have been clear to them that she shared their compassion for all things living.

Trusting and respecting their child also meant that Maya's parents did not hold her back. They allowed Maya to be part of the culture of the city where she was brought up. She was raised to fit in.

"In seventh grade," which would have made her about twelve years old, "my parents let me to go to the cotillion!" A cotillion is a formal, old-fashioned dance traditionally held to introduce upper-class girls to society.

"It was a room all full of white young people," Maya recalls. "And I remember the boys looking at each other: 'Who would have to dance with Maya?' Sometimes it was quite demoralizing but there were several boys who did dance with me. They were very nice."

From the rich complexity of growing up in a Jain household in the deep South of America, and then heading to the more diverse life of a university, along with time spent in communities of poverty in India, Maya emerged as unique person. That uniqueness enabled her to come up with highly creative strategies to address ills. Empathy is very much the hallmark of her character.

"It's a mix of things," she says. "I received a lot from my father when it comes to social justice and open-mindedness. My mother was also an inspiration—she taught herself English by selling Avon cosmetic products and wound up starting a computer consulting company. And their Jain spirit has always been fundamental to my way of thinking."

Maya not only founded the Global Fund for Children, she has written over twenty award-winning children's books. And these days she has taken her career to astonishing heights: as the President & CEO of Society for Science & the Public (SSP) and Publisher of Science News, she heads a large organization that plays a key role in promoting science education in the United States. It is through science, that has no allegiance to stories that divide us, that Maya is making a contribution to humanity that will reverberate for generations.

Having taken the traditions of India, filtered through the U.S., what she has become is really very much her own person.

"My extended family in India are devout Jains," she says, "but you know what? I may not be a traditional or devout Jain but as my father has said, 'If we taught you the importance of community, we gave you religion.' The openness is remarkable."

THE INVISIBLE WOMAN
Sangeeta Dey

Growing up in Varanasi, one of the oldest and holiest cities in all of India, Sangeeta Dey found herself both inspired as well as constrained. She knew what she was supposed to do and what was expected of her, but she also was aware of the as yet undefined desire or the inclination to be someone other than what people saw in her.

angeeta graduated from a private Catholic school, and completed a Bachelor's degree in chemistry and biology from a regional college. She kept well within the very clearly stated plan put forth by her parents—either get into a medical school or study engineering—but she was aware that she wanted something else for herself. Once, while sitting in a café, doing her laborious, repetitive homework, she overheard a conversation.

What was being said attracted her, deeply, and as the two younger girls spoke at the next table, Sangeeta looked at their identical, pale blue uniforms, observed their unconscious mimicry of speech, head tilts, slick and braided hair, and the way that they sipped their sodas through straws. She wondered about them as *individuals*. What motivated them? What held them back? What had they learned at home and from their families that put them at odds in society? What secrets did they keep of their truest aspirations? Would they ever be able to express themselves outside of conformity?

Then Sangeeta returned to equations and the periodic table. The work had a solid rhythm, inescapably so, and unless she hit the books daily for hours she ran the risk of falling behind. Falling behind meant that she might not fulfil her parents' plans for her or succeed in the classroom. The mere idea that none of it mattered in the long run, in terms of what she wanted for herself or what was in her inner core, was fleeting.

And those times when a sentence emerged and stood a chance of being expressed by her were not only rare, but uncomfortable also. Hardly anyone ever spoke up against his or her parents. And while snarky comments about the curriculum could be heard when the students were out of earshot of the adults, little or nothing was said to those in charge that might make them review or change their way of doing things.

"I was not good at challenging authority," Sangeeta confesses. "None of us were. That went against the way we were taught in India. The teacher speaks, the students listen, we memorize, we take tests. End of story."

There was, ironically, a great deal of satisfaction to be derived from following a plan, especially if it was rote and that a legion of others were in step as well. Sangeeta didn't have to indulge in introspection or worry about what made the most sense to her as a vocation. There were no options; college was not the holiday camp it can be in the United States. Having someone provide order, especially when one is a teenager, can remedy the scary business of 'Who am I? What do I want to do with my life?'

Like most if not all of her fellow students in Varanasi, the questions were answered for her. She was a good and dutiful daughter and she would become a doctor, preferably, or failing to get into a medical school, an engineer. Everything had been arranged for her, and within that framework there was said to be plenty of room for creativity and joy.

Sangeeta was meant to be grateful for the educational opportunity. She was supposed to get a sense of herself as a respectful daughter whose identity was wrapped up in fulfilling her parents' vision of her and the future.

Most of her classmates took up the task with vigour. Indeed, when they looked around Varanasi, at the scruffy tourists seeking enlightenment as well as at the local destitute, they felt privileged to have family support, intelligence, verve, and a mission that would lead, once completed, to monetary success and elevated social status.

The wondering that Sangeeta experienced did not define her, per se; it was more of a distraction from the purposefulness of her life. It seemed to get in the way of what her parents had decided was her purpose in life. She didn't welcome the advent of her skills of observation or the curiosity she felt when observing others. She also had no one to share these relatively private experiences with.

Her natural, intellectual curiosity was, in fact, an ironic burden because it enabled her to question a set of plans and values she was helpless to change. To try and change them would mean confronting her parents and her community, and that wasn't about to happen.

The idea of an intellectual passion was anathema to her classmates and her family. It made no sense, it served no purpose. It contradicted what was long established as the right way to do things.

The idea and plan all along were to construct a vocational path that would lead to social status and a degree of financial independence (but not so much that she would forget how she had gotten it).

To advance, top grades were needed, of course, the competition was harsh, and to push things along, Sangeeta's parents hired a tutor to help her in a subject that didn't come as naturally to her as the others she studied: Physics.

"Supriyo's father was a rather famous physicist at the university," says Sangeeta, "and my dad had wanted to hire him to be my tutor. But instead he suggested his son."

The two of them—tutor and pupil—hit it off right away, and in addition to physics, matters of the heart became part of the curriculum. Soon enough marriage was a topic of the conversation, which caused problems.

"Even though we were from the same culture and level of caste," says Sangeeta, "my parents were opposed. Because they had not been the ones to choose! They had wanted to choose my spouse for me. Which was funny because their backgrounds were so different both in terms of caste and upbringing. My mother is Punjabi, my father is Bengali. I spoke to my mother in her language, and I spoke to my father in his language. The one common language in the household was Hindi."

Sangeeta told me that her parents tried to stop the relationship. They blocked letters the two sent to one another—this was long before texts and emails—they kept the two apart, and of course, the lessons were over!

Which only fanned the flames.

Sangeeta is a slender person with long black hair, captivating eyes, and a great deal of fashionable poise. Supriyo towers over her and has a face that can be described as open and gentle.

"In the end they had to accept it," she says. "It was their pride that got in the way."

To keep the pride intact, Sangeeta was told that she could marry Supriyo, but wasn't allowed to let anyone in the family know that she had chosen him rather than her mother and father.

"They were like that," she says simply.

It's now twenty years since the marriage, and the dust has settled.

But when Supriyo decided that it was necessary to go to the States to study electrical engineering, Sangeeta didn't see this as the opportunity of a lifetime. On the contrary, she loved her family and the city where she grew up and was perfectly willing to fulfil her parents' expectations while tamping down thoughts that led her away from their mission, which was for her to become a doctor or engineer. Despite everything, she is loyal.

She had no support from her family or community to pursue anything outside of what had been decided already. The ambivalence, to say the least, that her parents had towards her new husband also made her feel guilty, as if she was abandoning them.

The problem was that love took precedence over fate, rootedness, and mixed feelings. Finally, she had to follow her heart.

In order to accompany her fiancé to the States, they had to get married. So they did, and in December 1995 Sangeeta arrived in Chicago in the dead of winter where she saw snow for the first time in her life. They then went to Champaign, Illinois, where Supriyo was studying.

It was bitterly cold, of course, that first year just outside of Chicago, but Sangeeta remembers being pleasantly surprised by how friendly everyone was to her. She would go into a shop or take public transportation and complete strangers would say hello to her, ask her about her day, and smile in her face.

"They smiled so often," she says, "that it made me paranoid. What did they want?"

She describes how people opened doors for her at shopping malls, gave her the right of way, and made her feel special. It was that experience of individuality that was new to her—not standing out as a foreigner or being leered at because she is a woman, but simply being seen as a person. It freaked her out at first.

She began to think of herself differently, and to imagine what it might be like to have conversations with people in which she could say nearly anything she liked. She could express a wish, tell a story, show interest in a subject that she had kept to herself back home . . . the possibilities were endless.

It wasn't just the distance from family that led her astray from the idealized future that her parents had planned for her—although that helped—it was the recognition that in the States no one cared what she did with her life or who she spoke to or what field of study ignited her passion. There was a demotic quality to everyday life that she was unfamiliar with, and she embraced it. She had been invisible in India, but here she was seen.

Subsequently, Sangeeta moved to Pennsylvania where Supriyo continued doctoral studies at Penn State. She enrolled as well, and enrolled in the undergraduate programme in psychology at the same school.

But in addition to her background in 'hard science,' which she had studied and earned a degree in while in India, Sangeeta decided to have a look at psychology. Maybe it was the way in which her own emotional life defined facts set out for her, or the wellspring of feelings that emerged as a pupil and then as a defiant daughter. Whatever the reasons, the subject hit a nerve.

"When my parents found out that I was studying disorders like schizophrenia and autism and so on, that it would 'only be mad people' who would come to see me, they shot down the choice," she tells. "They just weren't taking me seriously."

But it was here that all that tamping down finally ended. Sangeeta credits her spouse with giving her the confidence to end her allegiance to the past, and he has certainly contributed to her moving forwards, but from listening to her you get the sense that liberation was at hand, no matter what.

"Being in the States meant that I was not with my parents any more obviously and that I was free to do or be whatever I liked. Supriyo asked me: 'What do you want to do with your life?' No one had ever asked me that question before. So I thought about it, and I realized that I had been living someone else's dream. I began then to reprogram myself."

Sangeeta thought deeply about the curiosity she had always felt about the inner life. Observing others had seemed like a distraction, to be avoided, but now, on her own, she realized that this inclination was in large measure what defined her as a person. It was studying human behaviour that she was passionate about, and which she was good at doing. As a good observer and good listener, the segue to formal study of psychology in a university was natural.

She loved what she was doing, and her husband supported her 'hundred per cent.' "He said that I should do what I wanted. It was how he was brought up and he applied that thinking to me."

After completing her undergraduate degree, Sangeeta and her husband moved to Boston, Massachusetts, where Supriyo took a job and she pursued doctoral work at the Massachusetts School of Professional Psychology.

"So you can say, in fact, that my parents finally did get a daughter who is a doctor."

Practicing psychology as a young Indian woman had its own set of challenges. Being taken seriously was chief among them and while racism was rarely overt, Sangeeta did need to prove herself. She had not wholly anticipated the hurdle.

"I can remember the first time that I was in tears," she shares. "I was at North Shore Hospital in Salem and had just told a mother that her son had a neurological problem that interfered with how he processed information. He had not understood me when I spoke to him. But rather than acknowledge that what I was telling her was painful to hear, she took a different tack and put me down. She told me that she thought her child was a genius, and that was why he was having problems in school. So when I confronted her with the results of my evaluation, she actually said, 'It could be you. *I* have trouble understanding your English!'"

Sangeeta didn't respond; she took it in stride. She was resilient and insightful enough to understand that the woman was responding to bad news, but later she went to her supervisor and burst into tears. He smoothed things over for both Sangeeta and the patient's mother, but it was an incident that cut to the quick.

Nowadays, settled in the Bay Area, with an active bi-coastal clinical practice, Sangeeta puts things in perspective, and recognizes the value of her journey. While on the one hand she accepts the importance of self-discipline inculcated in her while in India, as well as the narrow and high expectations held of her by her parents, on the other she glows when speaking of the intellectual freedom she enjoys today.

"Frankly, I don't think I could have achieved the success I have had I stayed in India," she says. "I was able to appreciate interactive learning and the value of fluidity in reasoning skills here in the States. We don't learn by rote here; the teacher isn't regarded as a god. I could also apply myself to anything I wanted, and be anyone I wanted. Nothing was barred to me because of my caste, religion, or gender. I can be myself."

There are, nonetheless, unique and sometimes ironic challenges.

"I avoid seeing Asian families in my clinical practice these days," Sangeeta admits. "The problem would be often that the families come to me with a bright child or teenager who is doing well in school, but the parents are worried because he or she doesn't have friends or may not test well. The family sometimes is in denial about problems and when I mention things like

Asperger's or mild autism, they can get angry with me. Plus, they assume that because I am Indian that we share an automatic affiliation and the same set of cultural presumptions."

These difficulties complicate her clinical practice, and Sangeeta has had to adapt and develop versatile strategies for problem solving with the families.

"During the feedback sessions, the parents will often try to explain and justify every behaviour," she said, "which means that the reports I write have to be especially nuanced to their concerns, many of which are cultural."

Sangeeta's own struggles with nuance and emotional growth contribute to her patience and in her taking a long view.

"Many families call back two years later," she says. "Their son and daughter indeed has not moved beyond the behavioural difficulties I'd noted."

I wondered what specific inspiration and psychological imperatives Sangeeta had found in the United States. What, going beyond her individual achievement and struggle, might be of importance to others who are coming here, striking out on their own, letting go of the past, and trying to integrate what they were told to be with who they are and what they want?

As a psychologist, Sangeeta has been able to offer unique, professional insight into the process of achievement. She speaks of being driven, of recognizing her innate skills, of opportunities in the U.S., and of the great, good luck of being able to be free of parental and social expectations.

"Competing in India with so many talented people, and such limited resources is very difficult," she says. "Had I remained, who knows? I might not even have gotten into a medical school. But in the States there are so vast an array of opportunities and no one or no thing that held me back."

I ask her more about motivation since it seems to be key to her ability to focus. Both to accept her emotional conundrum as well as to *embrace* it and make it part of who she is.

"I feel as if I have always had an inherent drive to be able to do something," she says. "Right from the time I was born. I never quite relaxed, I've always had a sense of direction."

And how did coming to the States exactly play into that?

She says: "I wondered: 'What will I do here?' I recall being in the library that bitter cold winter in Illinois, far from home, able to be anyone I wanted, and thinking that I wanted respect for who I was going to be."

It was also being in a marriage with a man who fostered her feisty independence.

"Supriyo's parents were very easy-going when it came to raising children," she laughs. "He was such a good student, and so serious, that they allowed him a great deal of freedom. Plus, as I said, his father was a prominent physicist, and his mother, by the way, was from an extremely elite family from Calcutta. Their expectations were clear and obvious."

Being with a spouse who had the social confidence to pursue his aspirations without her having to monitor his progress constantly was liberating, and being in a country where she was unknown, where her attributes could be used as *she* chose, and with strong motivation, made Sangeeta feel that she had at last found a kind of tranquillity that she suspects would have been impossible had she stayed in Varanasi.

"It is a novel environment here," Sangeeta concludes. "I have no identity here. Which means to me that I want to be recognized. No one knows me here, my background, my caste, and, sure, people sometimes ask silly questions—strangers ask me about making curry—but I don't mind. My goal is to be credible, to be more credible than the person in the same profession. Because I am a foreigner, I feel the need to be better than all of the other neuropsychologists."

THE NEXT GENERATION
Saatvik Ahluwalia

The values and traditions of Indian immigrants, absorbed through having been born and raised in the mother country, clearly helped to inspire phenomenal achievement in the United States. Although those who came to the States before the 1980s were often physically cut off from going back home even for a visit, lives were enriched stateside in celebrations, cooking, socializing, and marrying within the broad Indian culture that had established itself here. When it became easier to go back and forth between the two nations, and to enjoy FaceTime or other features of social media, contact was deepened. The challenge for grandparents and parents who immigrated to the U.S. is to maintain for the next generation a sense of Indian identity while still encouraging them to fit into America.

How can there be this complex and at times contradictory duality? To be as American as apple pie so that one can lead Americans and at the same time be loyal to the values and traditions of the culture that provides the stability.

Saatvik Ahluwalia is a great example of someone who has his feet firmly in both worlds. Born in Boston, Massachusetts, he is a twenty-five-year-old graduate of Boston University, with his eye on a career in public service.

"I had been working on various political campaigns," Saatvik says, "and then when I graduated from B.U. in 2012, I worked with a small team that co-founded a certification programme called YouthTrade. Our goal was to certify young entrepreneurs whose products were making social and environmental impact and get them into the shelves of conscious capitalism companies such as Whole Foods Market and Nordstrom. We wanted to innovate 'the next big thing' that would build youth entrepreneurship."

But sustainability is a huge challenge for any enterprise, no matter how good the idea or plan. There were many challenges in this venture the biggest one was that the key Founder developed a chronic illness just as the certification was taking off and the project had to be placed on hold. This was sad and disappointing for the project, but it did not deter Saatvik from moving ahead.

"I was elected as Lexington Town Meeting member and subsequently ran for the Board of Selectman," he says. The position is one of five that acts as an executive board which makes policy and oversees the operation of town

Page 259: Stumping in support of Martha Coakley for Governor of Massachusetts with Governor Deval Patrick.

Helping students make silly putty at Lexington's annual Martin Luther King, Jr. Day of Service.

Celebrating his sister's birthday with the family.

government. Although Lexington is small—population thirty thousand—it is packed with a racially and religiously diverse group of professional and influential families with wide reach into other sectors and institutions throughout Massachusetts and the world. Getting well known there means developing a name for oneself elsewhere.

Saatvik knew that there were very few Asian individuals holding public office in New England, but that was part of his inspiration. He liked the idea of being on the cutting edge, and of doing something difficult.

It wasn't that people necessarily had a strong bias against an Indian in town government, but rather that Saatvik was a young new face. No one who looked like him had been a Selectman before. So even when he lost, he knew that one day he'd be back. *He did not take the loss personally.* He had at least made it known that an Indian could be part of the electoral process: whether it was him or someone else with a comparable background, Lexington's diversity would one day soon be reflected in its governance. Boston Globe noted his remarkable campaign and covered his run in a spread in the Living and Arts section.

Since his loss, his example, and election have served as inspiration for the Lexington Indian American community. When he ran, there were two Indian American's in office, himself included. Today there are ten elected Town Meeting members. "There is only one Indian American in government anywhere in New England—a State Representative in New Hampshire," Saatvik says. "But that is going to change."

Where do his ambition and resilience come from? "Both my parents went to elite private prep schools and colleges in India. My father graduated from St. Stephens College and my mother from Lady Shriram College—both rated #1 and #2 in surveys every year. They came to the U.S. so that my father could go to B.U. M.B.A. School—where incidentally he topped his class. They took loans to get here and when their money ran out—they lived and worked as household help at a Jewish family's home in Brookline to make ends meet. My father also worked at a liquor store and my mother cooked and cleaned for additional neighbourhood homes. So the work ethic and moving on despite all odds has been embedded in me through their example."

In addition his parents' upbringing gave him a unique perspective on life. His mother hails from a prestigious family with a history of highly educated members serving in education, medicine, engineering, and government service, while his father comes from more humble origins, where he and his four siblings are the first generation to be educated. What they shared, though, was intelligence, relentless drive to make the most of their lives, and to not let anything come in the way of their goals and aspirations.

Saatvik is also a global thinker, which is one reason among many that he sees himself as working in the public sector. He also draws deeply from the cultural background of his family those concepts that he believes he can apply to be a success like perseverance, hardwork, and the ability to not take things personally.

"I think that Indians are quite demanding of their children wanting them to be in 'professional' careers," he says, stating that he had a different upbringing. "In my case negative criticism was always framed in positive terms. This trait is fairly unique to my mother's brand of raising children. Most Indian parents are much harsher. My father too always asked me to follow my heart. Perhaps because I was raised this way, I've always believed that regardless of the obstacles placed in my way I can dust myself off and achieve my goals."

Saatvik goes back and forth logically between the values of his family's home, and the broader Indian culture. This makes perfect sense since his parents' values were shaped by the Indian environment in which they grew up and now they were living in the American cultural landscape. The two sets of values—the specific familial ones and the general ones from the culture— are about the same, which is a fascinating confluence. That confluence goes a long way towards explaining the unique psychology behind Indian immigration: in a broad sense, the Indians who immigrated to the U.S. carried with them cultural values derived from nationality as well as a highly individualistic interpretation of them. It was a consensus of the personal and political.

"My mother," Saatvik explains, "is a global leader in youth entrepreneurship and sustainability. She is a world leader in trying to resolve the crisis of unemployment among young people in developing nations. That's the background of achievement I have to compare myself to. I feel a need to go beyond that."

Whether he surpasses his mother or achieves at her level, the example she provides is irrefutable.

"My background as an Indian has me thinking," says Saatvik. "How do we legislate for the future? Indian culture in the States has led to success in technology, medicine, and finance—all fields that can be quite lucrative. But what about the innovation needed in government and public policy? Fine, it's not a vocation where one can make millions, but it gives one a seat at the table."

Saatvik's goals were outside the realm of his family's thinking in regard to his future. His father has an M.B.A. His mother has two Masters. His uncles and aunts could not see how he could earn a living as he tried to move forward in politics. "But once they saw me engaged in it," Saatvik says, "they changed their minds. They said things like, 'This kid wants to do something different!' And I got their support." Subsequent to the familial approval, Saatvik found himself surprisingly in a position that led others to believe his future was extremely bright. With the doubts erased, he was an object of great interest. He is taking things to the next level.

What changed immediately? "I got multiple marriage proposals right away," he says with a shy laugh.

GET A JOB
Poonam Ahluwalia

"The person you should be talking is my mother," gushes Saatvik Ahluwalia. "She's my role model and my inspiration!"

It's not every day that I meet a young man in his twenties who says that he wants me to meet his mother so of course I was intrigued. Poonam Ahluwalia is the mother in question, and even without her son Saatvik's enthusiastic endorsement, it is clear that Poonam is a person of magnitude. That she is recognized within her family as a person worth knowing added to her celebrity. I was already familiar with her name: In June 2013, Poonam was given the India New England Woman of The Year Award, in recognition of her work towards ending youth unemployment.

Bent the fact that her son had such outspoken respect for Poonam added to her lustre in a way that no award could. So many celebrities are valued by the world, but within their families difficulties can arise because the spouse and children may regard the person's time away from home as time away from them. Not so here!

"I was born in Jaipur," Poonam says to me, "and I came to the United States in 1985."

This placed her in the middle of the waves of immigration from India during a time when the intelligentsia were arriving in droves to further their education and escape turmoil. Poonam is part of the generation that came with very open minds, deep ambition, and less encumbrance than those that had preceded them. Their confidence superseded their doubts because they had been students of excellence in India. What the States offered were opportunities that had not existed at home.

"My husband had come here to study at Boston University," she says, "and I just came to see him. It was a long, difficult early time because neither of us had green cards. He was on a student visa, I was on a tourist visa. Our savings ended about six months into my arrival."

Coming from a top echelon family in Rajasthan had ill prepared Poonam for what came next, but she recounts the experience with vibrancy.

"Someone called from the Boston University student housing exchange, we had posted there, and said that in exchange for domestic work that my husband and I might provide, we could have a place to live and eat. We didn't have a choice."

Page 267: With Ismail Serageldin, Director, Library of Alexandria, at YES Forum 2007 in Alexandria Egypt.

With the YES team that organized the First Global Youth Employment Summit, 2001.

Recieving the India New England Woman of the Year Award in June 2013.

What Poonam describes was, as she puts it, highly unusual.

"It wasn't something that happened to Indians," she says, "because almost everyone I knew from India had private funds or jobs. We didn't. Because we did not have green cards, we weren't allowed to work."

The thing is that Poonam hadn't intended to stay in the States. She had been married five years by the time her husband left for New England, and the young couple had been separated about six months. It was supposed to be a brief visit, but it turned into something else entirely.

"I was planning to go back to India," says Poonam. "I had a good job there as a marketing executive for a large corporation, Pizza King, which I enjoyed. But I realized while in Boston that it was more important to support my husband in his job. He was getting an M.B.A. at the time."

Once she decided to remain in Boston, education was next on Poonam's agenda. She already had an M.A. in Political Science from Rajasthan University in Jaipur. Now to add to that a more vocationally-oriented course of study lay ahead. She enrolled at Boston University and completed an M.S. in Mass Communications.

"My education helped me to get the discipline to do whatever is needed," Poonam says. "I was able to think about and have the skills to develop the processes that would lead to the creation of an infrastructure needed for my plan to help with youth employment."

Global in her thinking, ambitious in her scope, Poonam set about creating something that hadn't been there before. It

With the YES Leaders from 55 countries at the 3rd YES Summit in Nairobi, Kenya.

With President Kibaki of Kenya at the Opening Ceremony of YES 2006 in Nairobi, Kenya.

was a wildly inventive and complex vision that she executed methodically and with exceptional focus. Combining the knowledge of poverty she had witnessed in Jaipur with her marketing skills and now her understanding and expertise in mass communications led to the development of a unique institution. No wonder Saatvik had urged me to meet his mother.

"From 1998 to 2002, I set up workshops on youth employment," Poonama says. "Around the world. To me it was obvious that this crucial issue was simply not getting the attention it deserved."

Her idea caught the attention of global leaders. Everyone knew that the civil unrest and ongoing violence among youth is linked in part to unemployment. When a young person has a job, and an ability to live independently, there is higher regard for oneself and others in the community. Frustration comes about when people live in the past, when they cannot see a present and future in which their labour has value. Poonam set about trying to coordinate efforts to remedy this ongoing global crisis.

"I put a team together," she says, "and we held the first global youth employment summit in 2002 in Alexandria, Egypt. It was a huge success. First Lady Mrs. Suzanne Mubarak attended with many members of the Egyptian Cabinet and Co-chaired the Summit with former President Clinton. Over sixteen hundred delegates (fifty per cent youth) came from a hundred countries. We had invitees and speakers, from the World Economic Forum, World Bank, ILO and other major development institutions, and every session had youth, women, and minority speakers. In about eighty countries youth created YES Networks, that would organize themselves to lobby government and UN systems for policy and programmes to promote youth employment. The Internet was just emerging and we made full use of the social networks to spread the word, gain momentum, and seek change. We were so ahead of our time."

The movement grew. The opportunity for people to meet others who were like-minded around the world, and whose hope trumped doubt, was irrefutable. So much despair exists within nations when the burden of meaningful social change with something as simple as getting young people jobs overwhelms those who ought to do good. What Poonam did was create an infrastructure in which people were able to recognize their strengths and to connect to others who had them as well.

"The next summit, which was huge, was held in Veracruz, Mexico," she says. "Others took place in Kenya, Azerbaijan, and Sweden in subsequent years. We set about creating coalitions and working with local governments—linking them with global institutions and funds."

As she speaks, she marvels at the optimism that the work created in the participants. People felt less overwhelmed knowing that solutions were possible.

"We set out to change the global agenda," she says. "We changed the conversation about youth around the world."

I wondered where her inspiration had come from. Not only that, but resilience. That Poonam had managed to think about changing a global perspective and had inured herself to criticism and adversity were unique attributes that others might acquire and learn from or use in their own endeavours.

"My heart would break when I sang lullabies to my children who were still so young at the time," she says. "I'd think of millions of other children who didn't have what mine had. That was my motivating force. Youth everywhere has the same aspirations, but not the same resources. How, I wondered, could I help to create that demand and those resources?"

Compelling about her philosophy is its realism, practicality, and well thought out schemata. Nothing is abstract about Poonam's approach to problem solving, and what she brings to the workplace are tools rather than just ideas.

"My mind works architecturally," she says, "I want to create sustainable structures."

As one example among many, Poonam points out a partnership that she developed in 2011 with Whole Foods, the grocery giant, to have stores in the North Atlantic region to partner in promoting YouthTrade certified products to— creating opportunities for young entrepreneurs. YES team created the YouthTrade certification for young people under the age of thirty-five years who had sustainable products that needed a marketing edge.

"John Mackey, the CEO of Whole Foods, came to the inaugural event," Poonam says, "and we had sixty young entrepreneurs there to meet him."

It was all becoming clear that Poonam's charisma, pragmatism, focus, passion, and ability to get the job done were deeply appealing to those who had the power to help her to realize her vision. But while she had identified her own children as the empathic source for her global project, I wondered what about her affluent upbringing in Jaipur had contributed to the project. She had grown up rich. How did that factor in?

"Living in India and having enough, I internalized it," she says. "I had abundance. And it would break my heart to see others who did not have enough. Look, it comes from my family. My grandfather was a big landowner, and he was also a philanthropist. He was a Hindu, but he helped fund the region's first Unitarian church. He donated money to all three religions! He got so many awards. And his education, too, played a role. He trained as a lawyer. He was the chairman of the local Municipal Board for many years in Shikohabad a small town near Agra. Saatvik didn't know that when he ran for selectman in Lexington, but he was like his grandfather in that political ambition."

As she speaks about her family, Poonam notes the development of social conscience. Not every family has so meaningful a set of values that it conveys to others within its grouping.

"I think it is inbred in my family," Poonam says, "it's just there. Most of my family are scientists, teachers, and doctors. It wasn't considered good to be in business. We were all about generosity."

That was the grandfather. He seemed to have acquired an iconic status. But what about the immediacy of her parents? What had their values and personalities contributed to Poonam's life as a global pioneer who hobnobbed with the likes of Bill Clinton?

"My father was from Agra," she says, "and he came from a very wealthy family. His father gave away most everything he had, he opened colleges, and you can still see buildings named after him. My mother's side? She was emancipated. She passed high school, and because there was no women's college in Rajasthan, where she grew up, she fought to become the first woman to attend a college that previously had been all male. My mother was a painter, and great reader. She has been my role model."

Poonam talks about her mother's mix of artistry and her valiant outlook on life. From her description, her mother was a cut up, one of a kind.

"She raced in car rallies," Poonam says with a laugh. "She won seven times and then quit. These weren't about speed, they were about precision, and she was just so good that no one could compete with her. And she was also adventurous about her style of dress: for example, she never loved properly covered sari blouses and always wore them backless."

Given her background, one which is rooted in regionalism, social class, caste, and family, all specific to India, how did Poonam raise Saatvik? He's an American kid, after all, which is what she wants, but how to make him Indian, too?

"Most Indian kids are not like Saatvik," says Poonam. "He's very unique. He has a great devotion to his culture. He is passionate about Bollywood dancing. He can read and write Hindi. We always had Indian food in my home; I didn't want him to eat just pizza and pasta."

The challenges of being Indian are not just there for Saatvik as he and his family work to preserve the past and embrace the future. Poonam feels that pressure as well. She speaks about what she continues to face in the United States as she moves forward in her work and life. For a person who seems to be brimming with confidence, what she said to conclude our conversation made me do a double take, it was that surprising.

"We carry around, I do, anyway, the values of colonialism," she says. "Americans make it much easier than in Europe, but it's there. The way we perceive ourselves, I mean. For myself it's manifest as a hesitancy to be confrontational with white people."

Combating the displacement of identity that continues to erode identity half a century after Indian independence is a fascinating insight and challenge especially so in a person as accomplished and on top of the world as Poonam. It is cause for reflection. The damage done in the past affects those who lack her depth, intellect, and resilience. It may be that the legacy of colonialism is part of why young people lack confidence needed to be ready for work. Poonam's insight into that predicament, and her own good fortune, make her uniquely suited to address the needs of youth who struggle in developing nations around the world.

MAKING THE CONNECTIONS

Sureshbala Bala Iyer _____

Few nationalities are global in their patterns of immigration or settling down, and when spread throughout North America, disparate in communities and varied in passions, what helps to keep alive their identity as an immigrant group? Within families and the specific places in which people find themselves, traditions, foods, festivals, and philosophies can create a strong and independent community. But how does one community maintain ties with others across the country?

C ertainly affiliations are maintained via relatively closed systems based on caste, region, religion, ethnicity, gender, and profession. But when Indians spread out around the world wish to maintain a broad sense of what it means and feels like to be Indian, in addition to these narrow categories, what mechanisms are in place to foster that?

The Internet is an obvious tool for connecting people; and, systems within this medium are developed, and are growing, to facilitate the process.

One global leader who has been highly successful in the endeavour to bring people from India together is Sureshbala Bala Iyer. As the former CEO of Asia TV USA, and before that the CEO of Zoom Entertainment Network (also known as the 'Bollywood Channel') Sureshbala is deeply familiar with and excited about helping to foster a way for Indian communities around the world to stay in touch and embrace the broad parameters of the culture.

Nowadays, Sureshbala is taking things to a new level. He's left New York City, moved to Toronto, Canada, and is starting a venture ambitious and original in scope.

"I'm trying to create a Netflix-type service for the diaspora," he says. "To have the most prolific number of Indian movies per year. Say, twelve hundred. The idea would be to create a subscription service for Indians around the world—through cable and onto the home T.V. The demand for content is high. What we would be doing, essentially, is releasing movies into home theatres. And these would be a range of titles, not escapist cinema. India is probably unique among civilizations in that

many homes are at least trilingual—this adds to a culture of content. By building this service, we are creating entertainment, but also a means of cultural support."

His fascination with and respect for culture inspires Sureshbala to have developed this business model. Sure, he's a business person; he has to be. But at the core of his being there exists a sense that without cultural ties between and within Indian communities around the world, much of value would be lost.

"There is a highly acculturated environment in India, but not in North America," he says. "So raising Indian kids here can create an onus for parents to respond to cultural needs. It's not like raising a family in India where fairy tales and stories and landmark festivals are part of ordinary life. We want to match what's on offer in India for North American families. Through this network, we want to show documentaries, and offer content that's not available here—floods, attacks. And Indian music! It's extremely diverse and rich."

A network of Indian movies stretching across North America, streaming into homes, creating a way for people of disparate backgrounds to share culture. What brought Sureshbala to this point? What about him as a person led him to believe that he could leverage his remarkable work as a media CEO into a worldwide company that could transform lives through cinema?

"I left India in 1992," he explains, "and for awhile had a pretty successful business in Dubai. I came to Toronto in 1998. The Internet was getting started, and I realized then that the levers that are going to control the next one hundred years are being invented in the U.S.—especially at the universities. I thought, too, that the pressure in the North American university system was such that I would not be able to get my kids into the schools unless I got them here early. So I took up residence in Canada and got my citizenship. It happened much faster than expected: I had heard it was supposed to take years. It took only six months!"

This was Sureshbala's plan for his children, but what did they think?

"It was a hard conversation to have with my older daughter who was nine years old at the time," he says thoughtfully. "I asked her about school in Canada compared to the one she had attended in Dubai. The Canadian school was not as rich. It wasn't five star. But she said, 'I like it better here. The teachers are better.'" She said much more, of course, going into details about the openness in the classrooms in Canada, and from the expression on her face and the sound of her voice and the way she put things, it became clear to Sureshbala that his views of education resonated for his kids. And it paid off. "My older daughter finished university," he says proudly, "and is now working at an ad agency. My younger daughter is finishing her last year at film school." Both kids take after Sureshbala and his wife, an artist and writer, in their interests and the direction of their lives.

Having the resources and ties, Sureshbala is nowadays back and forth between India and North America. He is really the embodiment of both diverse countries. Zoom Entertainment is based in Mumbai, *and* he has a future in media that is based in Toronto.

But I still don't know his personal story—where he was brought up, what sort of family background he has, what shaped him. So he tells me.

"I was raised in Bombay," he begins, "but I was born in Kerala with a Tam Brahm background. Growing up in Bombay, my family was exposed to the West, and we were quite westernized. We didn't ghettoize. Then I spent a few years in northern India. And a couple of years in East Africa, in Dar-es-Salaam. I moved many times, and at one time was in a different country every five years. I did business in Hong Kong and Singapore, always working with international executives. I wasn't intimidated. I didn't hesitate to present ideas."

But at last Sureshbala found a home in Canada. Toronto is, after all, a great place to raise a family—diverse in population, with a history of tolerance and culture, which is liberating. Free minds create new things.

"Canada was a shock," he says excitedly. "It was as if your entire history has been erased." He could reinvent himself. But first things first. "Initially, the Canadian experience was focused on getting work. Until then I didn't have to look for a job. I had moved so often. But now we had a family. I started an ad agency, sold it, and then left advertising to work in media. I was made head of the South Asia Channel at Rupert Murdoch's News Corporation Channel. Based in Mumbai." Sureshbala refers modestly to what became Asia's 'dominant youth and music network.' In the first eight months of his tenure, the channel went from third to first place in market share. He remained in India, in Mumbai, until 2010.

Running a powerful network sparked ideas that inspired Sureshbala. Combining his personal efforts around the globe to maintain Indian identity for his family with the tools he had been taught to use in media, he came up with the concept he spoke with me about when our conversation began. But this was a prototype.

"The initial idea was a content service for the diaspora," he continues. "The Canadian Broadcast Company, the CBC, heard me out. Look, seventeen per cent of new immigrants to Canada are from South Asia. The CBC needed to make themselves relevant to this group." And the Indians already in Canada. "The Indians in the Toronto area? None of them were acquainted with the CBC. So the CBC thought that what I proposed made sense: to introduce new immigrants to them. And I made that service for them by building the first South Asian 'On Demand' service, and it did extremely well for the CBC."

Picturing Sureshbala in the early years of his career in Canada, it's difficult to imagine how, in the most practical terms, he managed to put forward his ideas and have them resonate for corporate executives. But not only did they listen, they paid to see his ideas put into action.

"It took awhile," he admits. "I knew nobody, I knew only junior people. I met with ad agencies." He laughs at his former self. "The meetings went on a long time! People were helpful and happy. Then I'd ask for references in media and the Internet. The people who helped? They became and still are friends."

Sureshbala's persistence paid off. Before too long, he was meeting with top executives at the CBC, and things slowly got off the ground.

"I wanted to bring my experience and passion to this," he says.

But when Sureshbala speaks of creating a network of Indian culture, after all, what is it he refers to? What does he mean? Is Indian culture something that can be defined? Is it the same in North America among immigrants as it is within families who have not left home?

"There are two qualities," he says thoughtfully. "One thing I notice every time I'm in India is that Indians there are much more humble and respectful than here—of older people, of authority. The second thing is that something runs through our culture, which is that there is resilience, I believe. Wanting something badly and not getting it is experienced as a bump in the road. There is a belief that tomorrow will be better."

Sureshbala's own respect for systems and hierarchies enabled him to recognize sources of power and work confidently with them. His own resilience gave him patience; feeling that eventually his ideas would be put into action, he could move incrementally. He didn't need to have everything today. And it's the fluidity of his movements between the ancient and yet ever-changing India and being part of the immigrant community in North America that inspires him and keeps his ideas current. His efforts to stay connected, to define cultures, and to share ideas are what motivate him in the next venture.

"On the whole, our imaginations are very unsettling and challenging," he shares. "For us, who are first generation, we all exchange notes. Everyone is swapping stories, and feeling grateful for our lives."

Sureshbala is aware, too, of not just the heterogeneity of new immigrants from India, but of the broad spectrum of people who arrived in North America at various periods in history both in India and here. Different expectations, different skill sets, different reactions from both communities to one another, different laws. How are these differences important in establishing ties?

"There are three segments," he says. "The early immigrants, I'd say about forty per cent of the population. Who came from the 1960s through the early 1980s. There was a tendency then to be cocooned and to be ghettoized. And yet, this group is crucial: they are the custodians of family values. Then there are the 'ABCDs.' Or: American Born Confused Desi. They went to the same schools as the kids they grew up with in North America. They had white friends. As teenagers, there is a confrontation of identities among the ABCDs—they'll listen to Indian music, see Bollywood movies, travel to India to find their roots. It's somewhat of a subculture: not quite white, not quite Indian. Some are at the forefront of fusion: like creating hip-hop within Indian culture! Then there is the third group, the FOBs—fresh off the boat. They come with a knowledge of the homeland, and want to replicate the homeland. They are not assimilationist. So within this broad framework of three groups, it's very dynamic! It's exciting. This idea of creating a network across North America to reach all these groups is a journey of thirteen years for me."

Identifying what brings people together strengthens not just the immigrants themselves, but also the communities in which they find themselves. A secure and confident group of people has much more to add than those who are uncertain about identity, and who feel isolated. Sureshbala's youthful expressions of ties make the world a bit smaller. His own lifestyle of long years of nation hopping made him desire to create a network that would solidify his identity as an Indian and connect to others around the globe.

THE NEWS OF BUSINESS, THE BUSINESS OF NEWS
Raju Narisetti

Raju Narisetti, at the age of forty-eight has achieved enough for several lifetimes: managing editor of *The Wall Street Journal*, editor of *The Wall Street Journal Europe*, managing editor of *The Washington Post*, founding editor of *Mint* (the #2 business daily in India), and currently senior vice-president, strategy, for News Corporation. His reach is global, his reputation nonpareil. How did he do it?

A lot of his success story has to do with confidence, which was burnished by growing up in an intellectual home. His father was a newspaper editor, his mother was an English professor. Born in Hyderabad, Raju's path to becoming a world famous journalist took an unusual and somewhat circuitous route nonetheless. He achieved a B.A. in economics and sociology from Osmania University in Hyderabad and then an M.B.A. from the Institute of Rural Management in Anand. He worked then as a sales manager for a large dairy company selling butter and cheese. And then it dawned on him: "I didn't want to spend the rest of my life in management," he says. "Reading and writing were too important to me."

Recognizing both talent and ambition within himself, choosing not to ignore these things, he took a nine-month programme in New Delhi in journalism and joined *The Economic Times*, India's largest business paper.

While enjoying the practice of reporting, Raju felt confined.

"Professors were influential in telling me then to go to the United States," he says. "While they saw that they had taught me the nuts and bolts of reporting, what was missing were social and cultural contexts."

He was reporting events, but not fitting them into history or politics or economics so that everything was disparate; there was little interpretation and there was a rote, vocational quality to what he was doing. What Raju sought instead was vibrancy and a broader understanding of things. The *why* as well as the *what*.

He applied to schools in the States, and with the promise of financial aid, chose in 1990 to attend Indiana University in Bloomington, Indiana, in order to get a degree in journalism.

I wondered: why not stay in India? Yes, context was missing at work, he felt, in how events were reported. And, yes, the programmes in journalism tended to be more practical, he felt, than in helping students develop inquiry and an analytic approach. But weren't there more things to learn in India? Did he really feel he had to travel thousands of miles from home in order to develop the skills needed to become a top journalist?

"There are something like three hundred to four hundred universities in India," Raju says with a frankness that has helped propel his career. His honesty demands everything from himself and his listeners. "But the degrees given for journalism aren't worth the paper they're printed on. Most of the professors haven't stepped into a newsroom for over ten years. There are typically nine months to one-year programmes attached to newspapers. Courses are focused on teaching students how to write thirty-word leads. They teach professional skills and, as I said, very, very basic nuts and bolts. But there's nothing holistic about them."

Having left India with a solid education in business and a history of working in that sector, Raju set about becoming a journalist in the States. He was unflinchingly competitive and, more than that, he was highly focused. He spoke of wanting to compete and engage readers in English, and took pride in being new to the country and yet being highly capable of adaptation. To buttress his work, he took international business classes.

So it wasn't just the writing, but his expertise in a subject that helped to set him apart and ahead.

"I graduated from Indiana at the end of 1991," he says, "and was one of the twelve summer interns in the Pittsburgh bureau of *The Wall Street Journal*. I could really compete."

However, due to circumstances beyond his control, Raju's ascent was slower than it might have been. Namely, it was the beginning of a recession and, as he puts it, "No one was hiring."

Undaunted, Raju maintained focus. He says that by word of mouth, an editor reached out to him from Dayton, Ohio, and that he was recruited by *The Dayton Daily News*, owned by Cox newspapers, which at the time was the 50th largest paper in the country. He covered business, technology, and entrepreneurship, all subject areas just beginning to be noticed by readers as worth knowing about. Raju's business background, combined with his acumen as a reporter, served him well.

Part of what propelled him was the understanding that he did not have much of a Plan B. Whatever he was going to make of himself might be inspired by his parents, but there was no fortune, per se, to fall back on. His failure or success was entirely his responsibility.

"My family was very, very middle class," he shares. "Lower middle class, you might say. I saw that whatever I will become would be due to my education and effort. There was no family wealth, no inheritance. There was nothing behind us. What helped somewhat in that regard was having very liberal and encouraging parents, unlike many Indian parents, who accepted my decision to be a journalist despite journalism as a profession not held in especially high regard in India."

His sister became a doctor. He was unconventional.

"Most parents would have had a heart attack," Raju says, "with a 'I wish you well,' and, 'I hope you know what you're doing.'"

But he got emotional support and encouragement. That level of respect helped to shape his confidence. And it started early. Raju noted that the intellectual prowess of his home helped to make him comfortable around ideas, contexts, words, and engagement.

"My father got a half dozen newspapers each day," he says. "He also had something like eight or nine thousand books in the house." He smiles. "My sister and I had a game we'd play. We would sit next to each other and look at the shelves of books, and one of us would name a title, and the other would see how long it took to find it. It was, overall, an intellectually stimulating environment. We didn't have a lot of toys. And T.V. only came to India when I was fifteen, on the occasion of the Asian games in 1982."

So even though he lived far from the nurturing home he had grown up in, Raju took the precepts and imagery of that with him. Words and ideas were always a part of his self-identity.

Having a steely background—and the confidence it gave him—helped Raju persevere in the early days, twenty years ago, when faces like his were not as common as today. Back then proving oneself was an obstacle based not strictly on merit, but also on convincing people that even though one was unfamiliar in a newsroom, coming from another country, not looking like the classmates or neighbours of their youth, one belonged.

"In 1994, at *The Wall Street Journal*," he shares, "there were four Indians in the entire company. Now there are a few dozen. Back then I also joined the South Asian Journalists Association and we'd meet at a restaurant in midtown Manhattan. It was the organization's 20th anniversary in 2014, and we have twelve hundred to thirteen hundred members."

As he speaks of the early years, Raju is far from nostalgic. Throughout our conversation, he has shown pragmatism to marvel at. He speaks of slights he withstood, not taking them personally, but rather as synecdoches of a society that was limited in its understanding of the world outside of the United States and, hence, chauvinistic.

"I remember going to visit IBM in the early 1990s," he says, "up in Armonk, New York. As the meeting was getting started, someone said to me, 'You speak really good English.' I felt angry, but I didn't react, and I thought: it stems from ignorance. There's been a pretty significant shift now from those days."

What struck Raju was how much he knew about Americans in comparison to what *they* knew about India. It gave him, and others who shared his background, a hidden advantage.

"Look," he says, "if you're growing up in India, you have to know about the U.S. For a long time that awareness formed an envy of the West. But there's no longer envy of the West, and instead what we have is a great confidence that we can do it."

Confidence is indefinable, of course, you can't bottle it, it's not available in stores, it can't be taught, and at best all the self-help books, courses, and lectures can provide is a suit of armour you can place over a quivering bowl of pudding. The confidence that Raju spoke of is contextual and based on real events, economic and political, that might be inculcated by observers. His passion as a journalist enabled him to take relatively abstract changes in the world and internalize them. He knew, too, that he was not alone: India was more authoritative on a global scale than at any point in its history. The confidence derived from seeing many other Indians achieve greatness.

"The confidence I see in India is a combination of things," he says. "Economic downturns in the West. Rising unemployment in the West. Global terrorism. India has been fairly well isolated from the repercussions of these and related events, and a sense of confidence has emerged as a result. That's a big change from the days when I'd go back to India and hear relatives tell me, 'You've escaped.' I think that the envy disappeared in the late 1990s and early 2000s. And it's grown. In the last decade, for example, whenever I've gone to Hyderabad, local journalists have been proud of the fact that one of their own has done well here. They also see a lot of progress and growth within India."

The bipartite issue of India and the United States creates challenges for people like Raju. A U.S. citizen now, he recognizes having been shaped by an Indian upbringing. One challenge is to speak about his home country, the place of his birth, analytically while maintaining a perspective that sees how difficult it can be for a traditional country to change its ways of doing things.

"One of India's ongoing challenges," Raju says, "is that it is a very thin-skinned country. But things only get better if we are critical thinkers."

At this point, Raju's outlook is made even more complicated by the fact New York City is his home. His wife is American. His two children are half-Indian.

"I've crossed the line," he says. "I've made it hard for myself. I go back to India and it's not exactly like going home. *This* is my home. I'm not exactly willing to accept many things in India. Like being stopped by traffic cops for no reason and being asked by them for a couple of hundred rupees. I'm unwilling to deal with things like that, and I've made my life more complicated as a result." He pauses thoughtfully. "It's emotionally hard to be an expat in your own country."

What Raju identifies as the experiences in the United States that have led him to make this country his home are specific. He makes note of his home at *The Wall Street Journal* for about seventeen years. Of the pleasure he feels being in New York City.

"Working at *The Wall Street Journal* is the closest I've come to being in a meritocracy," he states. "It was all about one's ideas. Not: 'Who are you, what is your caste, what is your community?' You never get rid of those questions in India. At *The Wall Street Journal* it was, 'What have you done for us yesterday? What will you do for us tomorrow?' That's an empowering feeling. To be in a room of editors and talk about *ideas*."

Raju sees his life in the U.S. as a time when his intellect was recognized, and his ability to write and edit stories given the forum he would not have found in India. It's a bold view.

"The U.S. is a country at the end of the day where one's accent and colour don't matter as much as one's ideas," he says. "My wife is black and I'm sure that she has a different view of race in the U.S., but this is what I think. I'm given the benefit of the doubt here."

YAHOO!
Jai Singh

"I'm nowhere now."

The speaker is being somewhat ironic while also realistic and honest, but it's jarring to hear Jai Singh, the internationally renowned former editor-in-chief of Yahoo, based in California, speak of a juncture in his life that doesn't include getting the news out. What he says next is even more surprising.

"I am honestly so turned off by the whole journalism thing right now that I'm basically evaluating what I want to do next," he said. "What I might be passionate about."

As he speaks to me, Singh sounds increasingly like a person who has nothing to lose by opening up about his illustrious career running a major, global news service. Added to this honesty is his insistence that it is the news business itself that must come under scrutiny.

"The bottom line is that it's become all about the business," he says. "And one which runs in quarterly, three month cycles. Look, at Yahoo we had an algorithm. As editors, we decided what stories would run. Which ones wouldn't. The editors selected the stories and the algorithm then prioritized the order they were displayed in based on what stories were clicked on the most."

He waits, but I don't interrupt him.

"Clicks," he says.

For a man from Jaipur who built a career on *ideas*, the *notion* of 'clicks' offends him. After decades in the news industry, he is taking time off now to reflect on his future as well as that of journalism.

"We gave priority to what were the most popular stories, not the most important," he continues. "Which stories, which type of stories, got the most clicks. Kim Kardashian?" He laughs. "Lots of clicks! So the editorial content started to become determined not by the importance of the story as understood by an editor, but by the number of people who clicked it."

Singh grew up in Jaipur, studied business at college, and at about the age of twenty decided to expand his horizons and head to the States. The plan was to continue an education in business, but that soon proved to be unsatisfactory.

"I didn't like anything about it," he says. "But what I did like was how being abroad gave me the freedom and courage to say that. To say: I don't want to do this. It was different from being back home. Because in India the parents decide."

So the plan had been to boost his skills and gain authority by virtue of an academic path, but once he was away from family and community he had a chance he had not anticipated. Namely to follow his passion. That passion wasn't to study business. The fact that he eschewed business as a career meant that when the news *business* became *more* about business and *less* about news, he found himself nearly back where he started from.

When he first came to the States, Singh attended American University in Washington, D.C. He found that writing was something he was especially good at and enjoyed.

"But as irony would have it," he says, "a professor came to me and asked, 'Is this really what you want to be doing?' The thing was that I didn't fit the stereotype. At the time, not many Indians were studying journalism."

Singh pauses to reflect on the impasse between his discovery that he had found something to devote himself to and the discouragement he faced from someone outside his family. This wasn't his parents telling him what to do and what not to do. It was a complete stranger. Maybe he wasn't suited to be a journalist. Maybe his parents had been right, maybe they had seen something he hadn't.

"I went back to India for a visit," he continues. "It was 1980. My father had died. I told a cousin about my plan, my ambition, and she asked, 'Will you be able to put money on the table?' It was a good question."

Singh points out that at the time of his visit India had a socialist economy. The idea of entrepreneurship was foreign to what people were thinking, let alone doing. Singh's plans for his future didn't make sense to people back home. But he didn't get discouraged.

He returned to university and stuck to the subject about which he remained passionate.

"And I became the first foreign-born news editor of the college newspaper," he says. "I became the news editor of *The Eagle!*"

His pride in the accomplishment kept him going, but after graduation he couldn't get a job in the field.

"My cousin's prophecy came true," he says.

As he talks, his mood seems to lighten. He is describing failures, one after the other, but now it's from the perspective of phenomenal success.

"My first journalism job lasted four hours," he says. "I got hired to work in the bureau of the *Florida Times Union*. I got a Press I.D. I was second to the bureau chief. Me! My job was going to be to cover Capital Hill. This was on a Friday, and the job was supposed to start on Monday. I was on cloud nine! Then that Sunday evening the bureau chief who hired me called to say that the job was being eliminated." He pauses. "But that they'd pay me for the four hours I had spent on Friday getting things in order."

Everything that Singh speaks of makes his situation sound difficult and poignant. Implicit in his story was his unwillingness to give in to doubt. He knew he was a good reporter.

"I was going against the norm in the Indian community," he says. "I wasn't going into business or medicine or law."

Subsequent to the disappearance of his job, Singh freelanced for a while and then at last found work with The Source, which was a pre-AOL, online source for news. The enterprise was so enticing to investors that before long it was bought out by *Reader's Digest*. Singh likes to say that The Source was ahead of the curve, 'but too far ahead of the curve.' He seems to be implying that it didn't have a business model which matched its novel approach to reporting and distributing the news.

He lasted with the company 'four or five years' and then joined a start-up as the founding editor of a newsletter that he hoped would customize the news for subscribers. Distribution here proved to be a problem so he left and went to *PC Week*, which meant that he had to relocate to the Boston area, the publication's base of operations.

The longer he worked in the tech-news field, the more excited Singh became about the possibilities for reshaping how news is structured and how it reaches people. Naturally, this took him to California where the greatest innovations were taking place within a field that excited him and about which by this time he had acquired considerable knowledge.

What's remarkable about his story is how flexible Singh is in his ability to follow and create opportunity both for himself and the field of journalism itself. There was no career path he could take, there is nothing obvious about his progress. He was adept at identifying ideas where he saw potential. To do all these things during the period of the late 1980s when the Internet had not as yet been established as the future suggests a mind and will which stand out.

"I was lucky enough to get on the Internet bandwagon," Singh says with self-effacement.

But if you look at what he did, it's clear that he didn't really get on the bandwagon so much as help build it. He raised the bar on tech reporting and made digital journalism better than ever. He understood both tech *and* journalism. He was also operating without a corporate mentality. As a result, before long, Singh helped create the world's biggest tech site, CNET, now owned by CBS, as the founding editor.

"We were out hustling the big outlets at CNET," he says. "We were trying to be more timely than them. They were not as mindful as we were of the big changes taking place in tech."

The success of what Singh was doing attracted attention, and soon he was partnering with large news entities. Eventually, that led to Yahoo.

What's the future?

"Original content or die!" he says.

Despite the cynicism he expresses and his current uncertainty about what move to make next, Singh remains as idealistic as he was when he started out long ago in Jaipur. I ask him what advice he would give to a young person starting from India who wants to pursue his or her dreams in the United States.

"Go where your heart is," he says. "You may find that families back home will become more liberal as they see you develop. And, okay, you may not get into *The New York Times*, but take each day as it comes."

And why abroad? What is it about his life in the States that shaped and enabled him to succeed?

It's a meritocracy here for the most part," he says. "If you can deliver, you can get the job. I'm not sure that's the case in India."

THE PHILADELPHIA STORY
Ajay Raju

Many people choose a career path, relatively well-defined, and then set out to reach the goal. Others, restless and curious and capable, look to meet one goal after another. And in that process of discovery, these individuals keep changing. Altered is the schematic process by which a person is defined by the work. In other words, he or she is not an engineer, lawyer, doctor, politician, or business person, but rather is someone who knows engineering or business and practices law or medicine.

Not being defined by the work means that the individual, if successful, has a remarkable amount of flexibility, and can cull ideas and experiences from each aspect of his or her life. In that lifetime endeavour, the opportunity to create and envision what isn't there is extremely exciting. It leads to new things.

Ajay Raju is that sort of person: bigger than each of his jobs, and able to see what might be in the future. Even more remarkable is how he arrived at this point in his life. His journey, so much of what he has accomplished, and envisions, is extraordinary. As a corporate lawyer, CEO of a major law firm, and head of a venture fund, he sees beyond his day-to-day work and looks to a future that he intends to help create.

These days Ajay is based in Philadelphia, where he has become immersed in the city's vibrancy and culture. He is a civic leader.

"I came to the United States when I was fourteen years old," Ajay says. He is now in his forties. "I was born in Rewa, but living in Bhopal when I left India. My parents decided to emigrate for the same reasons that so many do: stability, better educational access, and a broader, brighter horizon of opportunity for their children. Raju speaks quickly and passionately as he described his interpretation of that initial passage. "Crossing oceans, I didn't know exactly what to expect when we came here in 1984. I didn't speak English. I understood it, but we spoke Hindi at home. And even though I faced that linguistic hurdle, something about America's essential vitality spoke to me clearly. Almost as soon as we arrived, I became distinctly aware of the basic qualities

Page 307: Ajay Raju with Thomas Sully's equestrian portrait of General George Washington at the Union League of Philadelphia.

Above: With members of the 2015 Germination Project Student Fellows class, posing for a *Vanity Fair*-style photo shoot at his Philadelphia home. **Below:** At a celebratory dinner with 2015 Germination Project Student Fellows.

that define America: open-mindedness, a sense of adventure, and above all, grit. I remember making a conscious decision to embrace those qualities myself and let them drive me from that day forward. Now that I'm a parent myself to three thoroughly American kids, I recognize that this spirit, which was so magnetic for me, dulls a bit through the generations. But I take heart knowing that as long as immigrants keep coming, it will live on."

But how did the family get permission to come here in the first place? Many people seek to immigrate to the U.S., after all, but significant legal barriers still exist. That in itself is an unusual and inspiring story.

"My mother's aunt was a nun and she simply told my mom to apply for a lottery slot," Ajay says. "We had no sponsor. We were lucky enough to get the slot, but without a sponsor, where could we go? What happened was this: a friend of our family, Abraham, was visiting at our house for dinner, and mentioned he'd heard about our situation. Abraham told us he knew someone in the U.S. who might be able to help. Right then and there he phoned this person, a man named Jacob, and asked him if he'd sponsor us. 'Of course I will!' Jacob said, and that was that. We had no family here, no prior connections, but that's how we ended up in Philadelphia—a chance dinner conversation and a five-minute long distance phone call! Either it was a random shot or something like destiny."

Once in the U.S., the family faced challenges, but the resiliencies of Ajay's parents helped enormously. "My father's degrees didn't transfer," Ajay says. "In India he was a high-ranking transportation professional. In Philadelphia he had to reinvent himself entirely. Initially, he did odd jobs, scrimped and saved, and eventually became a real estate developer. As for my mother, she was a nurse and found work readily in that profession. But other than Jacob, we didn't know anyone here."

Ajay reflects on that early period of change brought about by bold immigration. "Within a month, we were self-sufficient," he says. "All thanks to the sponsorship from a random stranger. It was a huge gesture on the part of Jacob to honour his friendship with Abraham, and we're grateful for it to this day."

Picturing the fourteen-year-old Ajay in a strange, new country seeking friends and academic success is more fully dimensional when he reveals yet another stumbling block in the path to success. "We came here in 1984," he explains, "and, as I said, I didn't speak English. Look, it was a long time ago, before the liberalization in India of the 1990s, before call centres and other outsourcing operations that created this tremendous demand for Indian workers who spoke English. Back then, only a handful of elites spoke English at home!"

Once in Philadelphia, Ajay, who arrived in the middle of the school year, entered the eighth grade, junior high school year, at a Catholic school: Holy Child. Did the rigor, conformity, and familiarity with the religion (as he is Catholic) help him to adapt? Not really. It was something else, funnily enough, that enabled Ajay to fit in. "Hair defined me in many ways," he says with what sounds like a pleasant, self-deprecating, and modest laugh. "I still sometimes obsess about it, and in those days I always, always carried a comb." Truth be told, he still has a beautiful head of hair. "So there I was at fourteen, arriving in a new school in the middle of the year, in a new country, and I didn't have a decent gel so I was constantly fixating on my hair. The other kids knew that about me and they would tease me." The teasing was affectionate and inviting. "I also had a natural curiosity about style. I looked and dressed different. I had my own style, and, for better or worse, I owned it. Maybe as a result I wasn't bullied." On the contrary. "I was a magnet. Kids would come up to me and ask me about what I was wearing: 'Where did you get that from?' That sort of thing. I was also an athlete, a track star—that helped."

But more than the hair, sports, and clothing, it was—and is—Ajay's attitude towards life that people find attractive. "I have always walked on the sunny side of the street," he says. Indeed, the more he talks, the more he sounds like a motivational speaker who has psychological insights of value. "I've always had a certain facility for navigating social interactions. Of course, the typical American high school is a social meat grinder, so I think having that innate confidence made my life as a teenage immigrant a lot less difficult than it could have been. Call it good fortune or survivor's guilt, but having had that experience, I've always felt a kind of moral obligation to bring everyone to the table."

Ajay tells a story of going to clubs in Philadelphia and being let in, but having the friends he came with excluded. He would sneak them in, through the back, refusing to allow the so-called velvet rope to be a barrier. He didn't want to be the only one allowed in—in anything. The social confidence Ajay had at the outset, which was fostered in his new school, helped him to build more relationships as he progressed through life both personally and professionally. He went onto law school, became hugely successful as an attorney, and developed a reputation for expertise in international transactions. Then he turned his sights on the city where he lived. How could his genius for bringing people together be useful here? "Philadelphia made me, it's as simple as that," he says.

Ajay saw outside himself and his community of origin, and although informed by both, has an energy that cannot be contained by either. Living in a major East Coast city of the United States, he had an arena then in which to develop his ideas, learn from others, and establish roots. For all its wealth and majesty, Philadelphia, especially at the time Ajay was growing up there, was a city held back by poverty and an antiquated infrastructure. His energy was perfectly suited for this.

"I don't know if my drive, and the way it was informed by my personal experience, would have translated in other cultures," Ajay says frankly. "My sense of wonder. My confidence. My desire to lead. I'm lucky enough to have been dropped in Philadelphia. Once you break in, it's an unbelievable experience—no one loves you like they love you in Philadelphia!"

Working closely with like-minded individuals, Ajay helped to establish a foundation that will help young people succeed in life. He thinks of it as 'venture philanthropy,' a project to fund and mentor people who show leadership qualities, but need the support and guidance of others to reach their potential. "We have surrendered the elemental concept of leadership that once defined Philadelphia," he says, "and we want to reverse that trend. Right now, Philadelphia's is a tale of two cities. We lead the country in child poverty, with a broken educational system, poor workforce development, and income inequality—we are in the bottom sixty per cent in these areas. And yet, we are in the top forty per cent in other areas: Comcast, a multi-billion dollar company, is based in Philadelphia. The city's colleges and universities grant more degrees than any other city in the United States. We have an amazing system of teaching and training for healthcare. And in arts and culture, through our museums and orchestras, we are among the top five in the world."

So what's to be done?

"Well, our contribution to the cause is The Germination Project." Ajay continues enthusiastically, "The idea is to create an ecosystem of leadership in our region by identifying, cultivating and unleashing our best and brightest young minds. We selected a dozen or so schools to start with three leaders per school; these are our Germination Fellows. The idea is to place our Fellows on a fast track to leadership. To become, in a sense, the 'Navy Seals,' of the region. The boot camp for these leaders comes about through affiliation with places like the Wharton School of Business, Penn Medicine, Jefferson Health System, the Philadelphia Museum of Art, and similar institutions." All elite institutions. Talk about lifting the velvet rope! "You could say it's 'the rich uncle factor,'" Ajay says with a laugh. "To act based on a belief in meritocracy. To have a fair fight."

Ajay goes about creating fairness in his practice of nurturing leaders, and is specific about how to go about doing it. "In order to create leadership, there has to be guidance and mentoring," he says. "But it's a reciprocal prerogative as well. We want the leaders we help nurture to recognize the value of the support they receive. So many leaders go to places like Miami, New York, Hong Kong, or Singapore, let's say. A basic underpinning of our civic philosophy, and a condition of participation in the Germination Project, is that our alumni ultimately commit their talents and careers to creating Philadelphia's best possible future.

Ajay's desire for and commitment to bringing people forward are seen in numerous other collaborative projects. He may have started in law, but what he does nowadays isn't easy to define as a vocation.

"I'm involved in bringing top contemporary artists from India to Philadelphia," he says. "The upper crust here collect art, and we want to create a modern version of a trade route. Not with spices, but art and culture. This initiative dovetails neatly with the Germination Project, as it's also committed to elevating Philadelphia's stature on a national and global scale. In the same vein, our partnership with organizations like the World Affairs Council of Philadelphia is connecting Philadelphia's student and young professional constituencies with national and international affairs.

These visionary projects and ideas don't mean that Ajay has neglected the profit side in his life. As the chairman and CEO of the Dilworth Paxson law firm, he has made a name for himself. As the firm describes him: "On structured finance and real estate capital markets transactions, Ajay has a top reputation in a broad spectrum of transactional areas, including mergers, acquisitions and divestitures, joint ventures, and cross-border strategic alliances. Recognized as one of the foremost authorities on issues arising from India's emergence as a global power, Ajay is regularly called upon by leading multinational corporations to provide counsel on navigating the Indian market, and to act as a liaison and negotiator within India's complex regulatory regime."

As part of Ajay's ability to see things with originality, he has added to the law firm's way of doing things through innovation. For example, he created a round table platform for multiple venture funds, including the fund he directs for Dilworth Paxson, to cross-syndicate deals and provide regional start-ups with access to capital. He doesn't separate ideas by differences, but sees their similarities instead.

"It's all about meritocracy; that's the fundamental concept at the centre of everything I do." Ajay says.

Which ideas have the greatest merit? Who are the people best suited to lead Philadelphia? "The way I describe it," Ajay says, "is let's say there are five of us stuck on a desert island and only twenty-four bottles of water remaining. We could divide up the bottles. We could say we're all equal. Or we could identify the person of the five who is the best swimmer, give that person the water, and have him or her swim for help, saying, 'Don't forget us!'"

Ajay's idealism came about for a variety of reasons: what he calls 'survivor's guilt,' his natural charisma, his genius for envisioning what's not there and the ability to create conditions to attain better conditions. Above all, he cites his parents as his inspiration, the two people who uprooted the family from Bhopal and took a chance on Philadelphia, which at the time

Ajay Raju with (from left to right) Steve Harmelin, Joe Jacovini, and Larry McMichael, members of Dilworth Paxson's senior leadership team at the firm's headquarters in Center City, Philadelphia.

was very much down on its luck. Their devotion is an example others might follow in guiding their kids.

"I had unique parents," Ajay says. "They constantly reminded me: 'Never forget who you are. Don't forget Abraham and the others who helped us. If you are a little bit stronger, use that strength to help others.'" He smiles. "My parents always regretted that I chose a for profit career. They wanted me to serve the community."

THE NEXT GENERATION OF YOUNG IMMIGRANTS
Siddharth Gurnani

Every generation reinvents itself. Facing new challenges, new ways of thinking and being, with far greater exposure to and participation in a global economy, the newest wave of young Indians arriving in America has an excitement about itself never before present in the same way by those who preceded. They are not as tentative. Better prepared to assimilate, due to their exposure to America via social media on the Internet, the latest arrivals bring bundles of energy to their experience in a new country.

Among the leaders in this vanguard is Siddharth Gurnani. Originally from Delhi, but living in the States for about nine years, Siddharth—or, as he prefers, Sid—came to study as an undergraduate and was smitten by the culture, the variety, the sheer opportunity of being whoever he wanted in a new place seemingly without limits. Having an open mind, he soon found that what he had started out doing wasn't necessarily what would be his future.

"When I came to the States in August 2007," Sid says, "it was to get a degree in mechanical engineering at Georgia Tech in Atlanta, Georgia. But that's not what I'm doing now in New York City!"

I ask him what it was like to show up as a very young man in the Deep South of the U.S. Historically, this was an area renowned for its conservative politics, which often included racist views and policies.

"How we identify and how others perceive us? Well," he says with a laugh, "we are such a movement now—Indians—that they recognize us for our brains. We're not seen as just running around with elephants."

The concept of intellectual reputation trumping cartoonish ideas of being a foreigner not only serves Indian immigrants well, it also contributes to self-image. Seen as brainy, they think of themselves as brainy. Valued for merits, they imbue meritocratic ideals. Ironically, being in a foreign place, so far from home where region and caste and religion matter so much more than in the States, means that individualistic aspects of

Page 319: Getting playful during the holidays over some freshly made gnocchi. In Santo Domingo (Dominican Republic) with friends, for an off-beat birthday celebration.

With his parents in front of the famous Mosque in Istanbul.

personalities can emerge. People are defined in the U.S. more by where they are *going* than where they are *from*.

"When I reflect back on what a telling change it was for me to come here," Sid continues, "I think of what it had been like to be sixteen or seventeen years old at school in Delhi. I wasn't thinking actively about college. I was just having fun. I had a great group of friends. I was doing well in school, but I didn't want to make a big deal out of it either."

His final two years of high school sound pretty ordinary. Science, commerce, arts. He headed a bit more in the direction of science and studied physics, chemistry, and math. But nothing leaped out to capture his fancy or ignite his passion.

"I really wasn't thinking about college," he says. "But what happened was this: a friend of mine in Delhi knew he was going to study in the States. He took the SATs. So I thought, 'I guess I'll take the SATs, too.' I did pretty well on my first attempt."

Sid is being characteristically modest. He did so well on the crucial SAT exam that he didn't have to take it a second time. His scores were that good and that competitive. But then he had a new problem. Having achieved scores that sufficed for U.S. schools, but with no preparation for or knowledge of how the application process worked, he had little idea of what to do next.

Sid's father is a graphic designer, and his mother runs a high-end travel agency for the top leaders of NGOs, corporations, and embassy staffs in India. Both parents were highly encouraging and supportive, but neither was familiar with the U.S. education system.

What to do?

"I needed help," Sid recalls shyly.

A friend suggested that he turn to a freelance college counsellor who assisted prospective students with preparing applications and liaising with schools.

"He helped me to commoditize it," he shares. "We developed a logistical outlook. We worked on essays. We looked for scholarships. And so on."

Together with his mother Anita, Sid went to meet with a representative of a U.S. university.

"The counsellor at school said, 'You'd be great,' and 'Go talk to him,'" says Sid. He smiles. "So mom and I went. We have this first meeting and I tell him my scores. He starts to sell America as a destination! He talks about the flexibility and freedom of a U.S. university. The extracurricular activities! The infrastructure. And then he says something that really resonates for me: You may start by studying one thing, but end with something else."

The monumental appeal of being able to explore avenues where his mind took him had great appeal. Having been brought up in schools where material was taught with an aim towards memorization and then a filter that would lead to the choice of a narrow vocational path at an early age, Sid must have been flabbergasted by the intellectual opportunities. He was being presented with the freedom to exercise his mind. And then, having stretched his intellect, he could decide where to apply himself in terms of a career. It was radical.

"I already liked the draw of a destination," Sid says. "I'd never been to the States, and had only travelled a little bit in Southeast Asia. So my first thought was: America is the destination. My second thought was: I would study engineering, as that field would be a natural progression from school up to that point."

He knew at the outset that engineering was the subject that would enable him to board a plane and start a new life. And that was that.

"In retrospect there's a reason why I don't work as an engineer today," he says. "It's not something I would have excelled at. For me it was always about the whole beauty of studying in the U.S."

As he speaks, the words tumble out.

"I'm a big advocate of education in the U.S.," he continues. "The internships where you can learn first-hand what a job entails. The opportunity to study abroad—I studied in France during the course of my time enrolled at Georgia Tech. The extracurricular activities. All these things work so well in tandem."

The richness and variety of the U.S. educational system at the college level freed Sid's mind and although he ended up with a B.Sc. in Mechanical Engineering with a minor in economics, he still hadn't decided what he wanted as a career.

"Engineering is a very valuable degree," he acknowledges. "It provided me with skills I could market. It's seen as a hard degree to accomplish, and it helped me to develop critical thinking skills." He laughs. "Although I don't do anything now related to engineering!"

The degree provided Sid with not just a road map, but also with a way to earn a living whether he chose to or not. In that sense, it gave him confidence. It's fair to say that it was something he could fall back on.

"But it didn't come to me passionately," he says. "I wanted to do something with people. I didn't want to be siloed."

Sid pursued his passion and after graduating from Georgia Tech, he found work with Deloitte Consulting. The company, one of the big four in the accounting world, and now one of the world's largest, provided Sid with exposure to the corporate world and it helped him diversify his skill sets.

"Officially, I am a 'human capital consultant,' he says. "Which means, very basically, taking a look at the extremely critical aspects of people-driven issues of companies. We look at things like talent strategies, organizational structures, human resource service delivery, and implementation. It's people issues that impact cost effectiveness and profit."

He began as an analyst with the company, but found that human resources wasn't really his thing.

"I wouldn't necessarily say I got out of the office and started on the job training as an analyst," he adds. "It was more that I didn't feel like I was fit to work as an engineer and working at Deloitte gave me the opportunity to express myself. The Deloitte job was always about working with clients and solving their human capital problems."

Out of the office, and training on the job and in the field, yielded powerful results for clients whose needs covered everything imaginable. He had to be fast on his feet, and open to shifting sets, thinking with versatility, and strategizing with an open mind.

Being open to possibilities, Sid realized that he needed to build on what he had learned in the classroom and on the job. He needed to come up with something very original that would enable him to cross the next bridge: What could he do to adapt to each new client? How would he able to respond to each demand or puzzle? One approach did not fit everyone, nor was what he had learned sufficient.

By this time, Sid had moved to New York City. Rather than sequestering himself and studying in conventional terms, he took advantage of what the city had to offer.

"I took an improv comedy class," he shares. "So outside my comfort zone! It wasn't about being funny. What I learned was that you don't have to be funny. It was created by the famous group, Upright Citizens Brigade, and what I learned over eight weeks was the art of improvisation. Which proves to be essential in consulting work."

Sid never settled for one accomplishment, and kept pushing himself to see what he might do next. He still hasn't tested his full potential.

Despite the success of having assimilated, of becoming an American, I ask him what he misses about India, and what nitty-gritty adjustments he had to make over the years. His efforts to fit in were not just intellectual. He is content emotionally as well.

"Well," he says, "the way people eat food here took getting used to. We share family style in India. The first few weeks after I had arrived, a bunch of us in the dorm went out. I had a thought of dipping my hand in someone else's plate: 'But you just don't!' You order an individual plate. That took a little bit of adjustment."

What compensated for the cultural shifts was the heady excitement of unfettered youth. He was eighteen, on his own, and free to become his own person.

"I didn't feel discrimination here," he said. "And although I missed my family, the excitement carried me forward. Things as basic as the fact that the U.S. educational system made me think. It wasn't like in India where you just read a book and memorize its contents. Here I had to think about what I was reading." He pauses. "That's something I had to learn."

The more he talks, the more his journey seems to have been planned rather than improvised, but of course that's not true. Sid's accomplishments came about through his willingness to adapt and to look into himself to see what he wanted. I ask him what advice he would give to someone from India who is eighteen or so and about to embark on university life in America.

"To be able to get an American education is such a great opportunity that you must challenge yourself," he says. "Do something you're uncomfortable doing. Make the most of it. My mom jokes in Hindi, 'You squeeze all the juice out a lemon.' I do. I worked for the college newspaper, I got campus jobs. Do everything you can think of. And to the parents who are sending their child off, I'd say, 'Let the kid explore. Trust that you inculcated the values and the upbringing. Don't worry if he's eating right. The best way to help is offer constructive advice.'"

With all that, I wonder what's next for Sid. Where will his dreams and abilities take him? He's not restless, but he refuses to accept the status quo. That's a mark of leadership not just for him, but for his generation.

"I have a Bohemian way of thinking," he says, and laughs again. "My personal goals? I'd like to live in a French speaking country for school or work in order to learn the language. It's such a beautiful language! And maybe get an M.B.A.—but on my own terms. I have a very open mind."

With his sister, Gayatri, spending time in South Carolina at a friend's home before a lavish Thanksgiving dinner.

Taking a picture with two children of a Guatemalan artisan whom he and his colleagues worked with while providing pro-bono consulting services to social entrepreneurs in Antigua, Guatemala.

SONGS OF CELEBRATION
Shilpa Ananth

Each year, more and more people come to the United States from
India, bringing with them hopes and aspirations, anxiety and dreams,
and in the process of their personal transformation, they cultivate and
join existing communities. With an infrastructure in place made up of
successful Indians, the newest arrivals have the opportunity to explore
artistic dimensions, not necessarily in traditional remunerative fields their
predecessors succeeded in. And in the course of their transformation,
they adapt to their new place by taking on its culture. They can add to
what they know and love. Nowhere is this more apparent than in music.

Deeply collaborative, and resonating with the rhythms of place, music is a way both to remember where a person comes from as well as a means to connect to a new place. Its ability to reach us neurologically is well documented, if not well understood, and as our brains change so do our behaviours, ideas, thoughts, and feelings. No medium is better at helping us see the future of Indian integration into American life.

"I was born in Dubai, but my family is from Kerala," says Shilpa Ananth. We're tableside at The Beat Hotel, a very cool and sophisticated venue and restaurant in Harvard Square, a stone's throw from the university. The opening act, a mix of seven musicians performing a blend of jazz and classical Indian tunes, is warming up the crowd. Shilpa has blown into town from Brooklyn, and will take the stage as soon as we're done speaking. "I went to high school in India, but came to the U.S. in January 2011, to study at the Berklee College of Music here in Boston."

Berklee is the premier contemporary music school in the United States with illustrious alumni like Keith Jarrett, Donald Fagen, Branford Marsalis, and Esperanza Spalding, among many others.

"My first degree, which I got in India, was in media communications and psychology," Shilpa tells. She's dressed to the nines as she is set to perform, but her demeanour is deeply serious as she speaks of music, her education, and her family. "Both my parents were born in India, their passports are still Indian, as is mine, and we maintained close ties with

Page 331: Shilpa at the Bedford Pier in Brooklyn, New York.

Performance of her debut album 'Indian Soul' release concert, at the Blue Note Jazz Club, New York, on February 13, 2015.

With her parents, at her graduation ceremony from Berklee College of Music, Boston, MA.

India throughout my childhood and adolescence. We went, for example, every summer to spend time on vacation with my grandparents."

Her father is an accountant, and her grandparents were traditional people, so the choice to commit to music professionally meant that Shilpa had to devote herself independently without early acceptance from her family.

"I always wanted to go into music. It's my passion, and at my core, but there was some pressure to get a 'stable degree.'"

Moving forward with her dream, Shilpa decided to study music further and more formally.

"Mount Carmel College, where I studied in India, is well known for its Arts programme," she explains.

"During my final semester there, I was researching music schools in the U.S., and stumbled upon Berklee's website. I found out they were holding auditions in Mumbai," Shilpa says, then smiles. "I don't know if it was the gods or fate!" Her dramatic style on a personal level lends itself to her ability to perform as a singer before audiences. "I went to the audition, held in Bombay, and I sang. Months later, I found that I had been accepted with a scholarship!"

What did Shilpa sing?

"I sang 'Bridge Over Troubled Water,'" she says, "but with an Indian twist. By 'twist' I mean that I made it very melodic, as if it was from an Indian point of view. I kept the lyrics the same."

Once she was in, she had to reckon with her parents. They had never been to the States, and were not behind the decision of their young daughter to come here solo.

"It took a year to convince them," she tells frankly. Like all serious artists, Shilpa comes across as honest about her life. "They finally came around and let me go." She laughs again, then takes a sip of ice water before returning the glass to the table's gleaming surface. "I had do a PowerPoint presentation to my parents! They really are very traditional. I had to convince them."

Before coming to study formally at Berklee, Shilpa had practiced and tried to perfect her craft. Her focus is impressive, and her mix of logic and art convincing.

"In India and Dubai, I performed all across the board," she says. "Western settings. Pageants. Competitions—in Dubai, when I was fourteen, I entered The Best of the Best. I didn't win, but I did it! I was also in spiritual settings: I performed in temples: the Hindu version of gospel, which we call *bhajans*. So early on, my parents knew that I could do it. My father would hear from people, 'Wow, your daughter can sing!'"

Once at Berklee, Shilpa expanded her horizons by embracing new forms of music. She added to what she knew and loved, and became better for her efforts.

"I loved being at Berklee," she gushes. "Great students. New music: Bulgarian, Andalusian, jazz! It was the worst winter in Boston, some said, but it was a great environment."

As Shilpa progressed in her personal and musical education, how was she able to weave together the strands of her life *before* arriving in the States with all that was new here? She is quintessentially Indian, from a traditional family, and yet she is open to the world.

"I always felt connected to Western music as well as Indian," Shilpa says. "And people here also want to listen to music from India. The thing, too, is: I'm not here to be the 'biggest Indian' on the whole globe! I'm here to learn other music and incorporate it into my music. Which I did. Jazz licks, Blues scales—both with my own twist. It's East meets West. Fusion music that is still true to my roots. I don't stick to one category or one genre."

It's Shilpa's feisty personality, with her ability to focus on developing her talent, that has enabled her to put together a musical identity. That identity is a real transformation and while it's likely that it wouldn't have happened quite so readily outside of the States—had she stayed in India or Dubai—she is fundamentally who she always was.

"I've always been a rebellious person," she says. "If not, I might as well be back home." Part of that rebellion led her to leave Boston for New York City. "It was definitely a big change. I'd been in Boston three and a half years. But for my career, I moved to Brooklyn. I didn't know anyone in Brooklyn. I started from scratch." Her verve gives way momentarily to a degree of introspection. "It's hard," she reflects. "I think of leaving the business sometimes. I ask myself: 'Should I just go back? Should I just give up?' It can be a daily struggle."

But Shilpa's commitment to her work keeps her going. She just released her first album, *Indian Soul*, and is out promoting it on tour at festivals and clubs nationwide. With cover art showing on one side a hand with henna tattoo and on the other a photo of Shilpa's smiling face in what seem to be fragments, and with songs that have titles such as, 'Feels so natural', 'Dream race', and 'Enge nee', it's a great expression of the amalgam of Shilpa's personality and artistry.

"I'm definitely not entirely Indian," she says.

When we have concluded our talk for the evening, and the set is cleared from the opening act, and new instruments brought to the stage, accompanied by musicians, Shilpa gets up and walks up to the microphone. From the first words, her voice takes hold of the audience. She sings with what seems to be hesitancy, but after the first song, her confidence imbues the sounds with depth and a haunting sense of belonging as well as yearning. Many years ago, Led Zeppelin performed 'Immigrant Song,' and Shilpa's voice makes me think of that plangent sound. Only she does it better . . . Her song suggests a future in America unimaginable without a past in India.

AFTERWORD

—————◆—————

What have we learned? Thirty prominent
Indians living across America, with diverse
backgrounds, origins, goals, and viewpoints,
have opened their hearts and minds. In story
after story, the precise details of people's
resilience and versatility have shown what
it takes to make it in a radically new place.
The United States has many things it shares
with India, but ultimately its differences
require enormous stamina and focus from
immigrants in order to succeed here. While

the opportunities for making a fortune, raising vibrant and healthy children, and getting a first-rate education are vast in the U.S., so, too, is the likelihood of failure. It is a tough place, the States, where money matters more than many places on earth, and where politically correct talk can insidiously mask injustice.

To understand better what we have learned from the stories told, look first to what people sought. The expectations of Indian immigrants, over the past fifty years, vary enormously. Depending on when people came here, it could be the desire for physical safety that was a paramount expectation. Or, it might be access to higher education, better jobs, a clean environment, a government that is accountable and punishes corruption, an economic climate unfettered by government control and regulation, a wish to contribute to global well-being, and a highly personal wish to create a self that isn't limited by parental, gender, caste, or class expectations. Few places on earth offer people the chance to reinvent oneself and fit in with the existing society.

The wonderful contradictions between a society which monetizes nearly everything as well as a culture in which personal liberation isn't just possible but encouraged, makes living in the United States extremely exciting at this period in world history.

No matter when people arrived in the United States from India, it is clear that many sought the same things, which were felt to be most accessible in this country.

Freedom to create. People spoke about a need and desire to use the imagination to do things in ways that had not been done before. Whether it was using the Internet to create global networks between Indian families through streaming video, or becoming a stand-up comedian by telling intimate stories about one's family, immigrants feel that it is here in the States that creativity is given the greatest impetus. Combining academic disciplines, building coalitions with people whose affiliations are based on ideas, rather than religion or caste, make creativity a broader based possibility. Ideas come from many sources rather than within the traditional sets of affiliation from back home.

More flexibility. Whether it was to pursue undergraduate education that included many different subjects or a vocation that used ideas from more than one field, immigrants have a chance to explore interests and put together seemingly disparate approaches to problem solving. Originality in analytical thinking is sought, and so are opportunities to participate, through questions, in work and school settings. People want to experience life and contribute to discussions not through rote repetition or accepted truth, but by saying what they think or feel without fear of criticism. The purpose is to acquire knowledge by trying things out that have not been tried before.

Idealism. Immigrants repeatedly spoke of recognizing ideals in the United States—justice, freedom—and more or less demanded that their new home live up to these ideals. It can't just be on paper, it has to be true, and it has to be lived.

Assimilation. As loyal as immigrants are to their affiliations from home—caste, region, religion—there exists, also, a strong desire to be American as well as Indian. People don't want to live in separate communities and restrict friendships and business ties just to other Indians, in general, and certainly not to their highly specific background. In order to benefit most from life in North America, to fit in, immigrants want to do many of the same things their non-Indian neighbours are doing. It's not to give up the past (although it can mean that), but to add to it. Hence, we see famous Indian CEOs, managing editors, surgeon generals, and writers.

Education. The great number of top institutions in the U.S. means that many highly qualified Indians have found a way to deepen their knowledge of how the world works. Seeking out the best programmes and professors, taking on the hard work of delving deeply into a subject, is more possible in the U.S. due to the vastness of its first-rate university system.

Entrepreneurial Opportunities. Meeting like-minded, adventurous risk-takers whose well-capitalized ventures trump fear isn't that unusual an experience in the States. In the major cities, deals are being made left and right between relative strangers, banks loan huge sums of money with little collateral put up, and who someone is (their background) matters far less than whether others are convinced that they can make money from that person's ideas. This is very appealing to immigrants.

Minimizing Conflict. Coming from a country where, frankly, one's caste, class, religion, gender, region, or race can be a barrier to success, immigrants seek to live in a place where these artificial constructs are minimized. The point is to come to a place where one's ideas matter, but even more importantly where one's character is central to social interaction. The freedom that comes from being oneself, not judged by others who think they know who you are based on your name, speech, or appearance is profoundly life-changing.

And what do people bring with them from India? What special attributes aid in gaining success? Indians aren't smarter than anyone else. There is no genetic code to achievement. Nor are children being brought up in magically formulaic homes in which the way that parents raise them makes them more likely to come out on top. In fact, statistically there are far more failures in *any* field or country or group than there are successes. So what accounts for the achievement thus far of this remarkable group of people?

Family Support. In most instances, immigrants from India who succeed in the U.S. have unusually strong emotional support from a family member. It might take time—a PowerPoint presentation—but ultimately a father or mother stepped forward to embrace or even bless the decision to move, marry, or choose a career. Even though the immigrant has left family behind, that support matters enormously to building self-confidence. The support robs the experience of feeling like a betrayal of the family's values, and reframes it. With the support, the immigrant feels as if he or she is carrying on a family tradition. Trust has been given.

Caste Expectations. For many people, coming from a caste in which academic life, appreciation for economic policy, respect for women, or involvement in commerce meant that the person grew up expecting to follow on some significant path. He or she knew other family or caste affiliates who had succeeded in